Touring Gotham's Archaeological Past

Touring Gotham's Archaeological Past

8 Self-Guided Walking Tours through New York City

Diana diZerega Wall & Anne-Marie Cantwell

YALE UNIVERSITY PRESS NEW HAVEN & LONDON

Published with assistance from the Kingsley Trust Association
Publication Fund established by the Scroll and Key Society of
Yale College.

Designed by Nancy Ovedovitz and set in The Sans type
by BW&A Books, Inc. Printed in the United States of America
by R. R. Donnelley.

Library of Congress Cataloging-in-Publication Data
Wall, Diana diZerega.
Touring Gotham's archaeological past : eight self-guided
walking tours through New York City / Diana diZerega Wall
and Anne-Marie Cantwell.
p. cm.
Includes bibliographical references and index.
ISBN 0-300-10388-3 (pbk. : alk. paper)
1. Walking—New York Region—Guidebooks. 2. New
York Region—Antiquities. 3. Historic sites—New York Re-
gion. 4. New York Region—History, Local. 5. New York
Region—Tours. I. Cantwell, Anne-Marie E., date. II. Title.
F128.39.W357 2004
917.47'10444—dc22   2004005084

A catalogue record for this book is available from the
British Library.

The paper in this book meets the guidelines for permanence
and durability of the Committee on Production Guidelines for
Book Longevity of the Council on Library Resources.

10   9   8   7   6   5   4   3   2   1

Acknowledgments

We could not have written this book of tours without the work of our colleagues, who contributed in many important ways to the study of the city's past. First, we are grateful to those dedicated archaeologists, both professional and avocational, who worked in New York in the early and mid-twentieth century, when most professional archaeologists were engaged elsewhere. Without their hard and often unsung labor, we would know much less about New York's past, particularly the millennia of Native American life.

For discussing their own work with us or for reading and commenting on sections of the manuscript that covered their work, we thank H. Arthur Bankoff, Eugene Boesch, Laura Chmielewski, David Conlin, Evangeline Egglezos, Robert Fitts, James Garman, Joan Geismar, Petar Glumac, William Griswold, Richard Holmes, Richard Hunter, Terry Klein, Alyssa Loorya, James Moore, Mary Anne Mrozinski, Daniel Pagano, Michael Pappalardo, William Parry, Arnold Pickman, Lynn Rakos, Christopher Ricciardi, Nan Rothschild, Sean Sawyer, Chuck Smythe, Linda Stone, and Amanda Sutphin. We are also grateful to David Hurst Thomas and Lori Pendleton for discussing with us the ethical issues involved in writing archaeological tour books. It is a pleasure to have such good and generous colleagues.

Many colleagues were particularly generous in providing illustrations. We wish to thank Sean Asby, Kenneth Cobb, Deborah Cox, David Conlin, Diane Dallal, Karen Flinn, Anna French, Joan Geismar, Edith Gonzalez de Scollard, Pamela Greene, William Griswold, Herbert Kraft, Alan Leveillee, Christopher Ricciardi, Daniel Roberts, Nan A. Rothschild, Margy Schoettle, and Lorraine Williams.

We also thank Beverly Lucas and Barbara Johnson of the Anthropology Department of the City College of New York and Dawn Wilson of the Anthropology Department of Rutgers University–Newark for help along the way.

Our association with Yale University Press continues to be a pleasure. First and foremost, we thank Harry Haskell, our superlative editor. He suggested that we write this book, and his enthusiasm saw us through to its completion. We are also grateful to Lauren Shapiro, who assumed the editorship of this book in its final stages and whose expertise saw it through its publication. We thank Jenya Weinreb, our manuscript editor, for her invaluable help. Additional thanks go to Erik Kolb and Matthew Weston for help in rounding up the illustrations and permissions. We are grateful to Mary Traester, who traveled throughout the city with us, taking the photographs that form most of the frontispieces for the tours. We also thank Bill Nelson, who drafted the maps, and our designer, Nancy Ovedovitz, for making the book so attractive.

Last but not least, we thank our families, without whose support and patience we never would have finished this project.

ACKNOWLEDGMENTS

Introduction

When our book *Unearthing Gotham: The Archaeology of New York City* was published a few years ago, we weren't sure what its reception would be. As it turned out, we were overwhelmed by all the favorable attention that it, and we, received. But everyone asked the same question: "What sites can we go and see?" We thought about it, got out our maps and notebooks, put on our comfortable shoes, took buses and subways all over town, and came up with this book of explorations, our answer to that question. We had a wonderful time plotting these expeditions so that you could see the city of New York in a different way, as we archaeologists do.

The construction of these tours gave us the chance to talk about a number of archaeological sites that we love but were not able to fit into *Unearthing Gotham*. It also gave us a chance to revisit some of our favorite sites. But amazingly, in many cases the tours took us to parts of the city where we had never been during all the decades that we have lived in New York. How fascinating and wonderful those neighborhoods are! We were reminded over and over again what an extraordinary city New York is and was.

We recommend this book to anyone interested in New York. Whether you are an inveterate New Yorker or a tourist visiting for only a short time, the tours will give you a new slant on the city's past and present. Before you explore the city, though, you might want some background about the people connected to the sites you are going to see—both the inhabitants who lived there and the archaeologists who excavated the sites. You'll be walking in all of their footsteps.

The City and Its People

The peopling of New York began 11,000 years ago with the arrival of the first Native Americans, a people archaeologists call Paleoindians. For millennia thereafter, New York was Indian country. Archaeologists have divided those many centuries into a number of periods. The Paleoindians lived here for around a thousand years, from 11,000 to 10,000 B.P. ("before present"). These first New Yorkers adapted to what was then a harsh inland area, a hundred miles from the coast, at the end of the last Ice Age. Next came the Archaic peoples, who lived here between 10,000 and 2,700 B.P. At the beginning of this time the area was still inland, but by its end, sea levels had risen to their present stance and the coast was much as it is today. Then came the Woodland peoples, who were here from 2,700 to 400 B.P. Theirs were times of great technological innovation and a very successful adaptation to the incredibly rich marine environment around the city's coast, a bounty that made possible a distinctive way of life.

By the end of the Woodland period, we can at last put names to the people here and to the land we now call New York. We know that they were an Algonquian people, part of a larger group sometimes known as Delaware or Lenape. They spoke a dialect called Munsee and had ties with other Munsee speakers across Lenapehoking, a territory stretching from the lower Hudson to western Long Island, northern New Jersey, and northeastern Pennsylvania. But the Munsees did not form a single political unit; they were simply a number of independent, autonomous groups whose leaders led by persuasion. Some of the names of these groups and their settlements still resonate in the place-names of the modern metropolitan area —Canarsie and Manhattan—while others—Rechgawawank, Siwanoy, and Wiechquaeskect—are all but lost to the modern ear.

Throughout these long centuries, the Atlantic coast was a formidable barrier. But in the seventeenth century, Europeans and Africans arrived in Indian country; the coast was no longer a barrier, but became a conduit to and from the "Old World." The meetings of these peoples from three different continents, each with their own traditions and diseases, brought about dramatic changes that, for better and for worse, created a "New World" in a world already old, and eventually led to the establishment of New York City. By the end of the century, most of the Native Americans had been displaced from their homeland and had begun their own journeys west. Their descendants are now living all over the continent, especially in Oklahoma, Canada, and Wisconsin.

The seventeenth century first brought the Dutch, who were lured by the possibilities of trade in furs, and then the English, who wanted to consolidate their colonial holdings in North America to encompass the whole Atlantic coast from New England to the Carolinas. Both colonial powers depended heavily on the labor of enslaved Africans to build the city. The English continued in power until the Revolutionary War, leaving only after occupying the city for the war's duration. After the war, New York became the premier port of the new nation, a position it held for a century and a half, with its strong economy attracting millions of migrants and immigrants alike. As the city thrived, wage labor replaced slave labor, and emancipation finally came to the city in 1827. New York's population soared as it became a major manufacturing center and, later, a world financial and information center.

Because of its long and varied natural and cultural history, New York is a major archaeological site. The artifacts found beneath the city, at the sites that you will visit, underscore the many and diverse routes that all its inhabitants followed, each path leading in its own way to the creation of the modern city of New York. On these tours, you will discover the hidden Native American past, most of which can be explored only through archaeology. You will see sites where archaeologists have discovered evidence of the earliest New Yorkers, of thousand-year-old trading routes, of sacred burial grounds, and of dogs buried as humans were. You will also visit sites where archaeologists have uncovered the lives of colonial farmers, enslaved Africans, Revolutionary War soldiers, and nineteenth-century hotel keepers, grocers, and housewives. You will see where archaeologists found scuttled ships and revealed the secrets of early land filling. And you will also learn about the archaeologists themselves.

The Archaeologists

On these tours, you will meet some of the archaeologists who have been excavating the remains and recording the stories of the many peoples who once lived here. They, too, have a history, one that begins more than a hundred years ago when some of the first professional archaeologists in the country dug here briefly for local museums. But from the first decades of the twentieth century until the 1970s, professional archaeologists worked in New York only rarely. During that long period of professional neglect, self-trained avocational archaeologists struggled to save the relics of the city's past. They worked in an era when hundreds of the city's archaeological sites were being destroyed by urbanization. Without their dedication, we would know relatively little about the city's long Native American history.

With the passage of environmental legislation in the 1960s and 1970s, professional archaeologists began to work in the city again. This legislation, which now exists on the federal, state, and local levels, requires that under certain circumstances, when the government is involved in a construction project, a study must be made to determine the impact of that project on archaeological sites. If an important site is endangered, the construction project might be stopped or redesigned, or, in most cases, the site might be excavated by trained professionals paid by the developer. These archaeologists may work for large engineering or environmental firms or be self-employed as consultants. Their work is mandated, and it is overseen by archaeologists who work in government agencies. If much of what we know about the city's Native American past was learned in the early days by avocational archaeologists, much of what we have discovered archaeologically about the more recent past—about colonial New York, slavery, life in the slums and the suburbs, and the development of the global economy —was unearthed by this new generation of archaeologists who came armed with modern techniques and an interest in studying the city's more recent, as well as its older, past.

It is the work of all of these archaeologists together, professional and amateur alike, excavating with state-of-the-art methods or early twentieth-century techniques, that allows us to present to you a very different New York story than the one covered by the media today. It is a dramatic story of changing environments and landscapes and a panoramic view of the countless generations of people who have lived here over the past 11,000 years.

Getting There

Although you can drive along most of these routes, we have designed all but one of them as walking tours. The one exception is the first tour, of New York Harbor, where you go by ferry. In cases where sites are fairly far apart, we have provided directions for traveling by the city's buses. From the high perch of a bus seat, much more than from the lower vantage point of a car or taxicab, you can see the city's neighborhoods in all their variety and easily imagine them as they once were. (Note that buses accept either exact change in coins or Metrocards, available at any subway station.) Directions for each tour bring you to the first tour stop, take you through the entire tour, and then lead you home again. Be sure to read through each tour before you take it. Because some of the smaller museums are open irregularly, always call ahead to check on their hours.

The Tours

The eight self-guided tours or expeditions in this book will lead you to several very different New Yorks. You will explore largely unknown aspects of New York's distant past, but at the same time you will explore the modern city. And in some cases, you will also explore the city at the beginning of the twentieth century, as it was becoming urbanized and as the intrepid early archaeologists, professional and avocational alike, rushed to save its past. Some of these sites are near popular tourist attractions, while others are in places that even the most seasoned New Yorkers have never seen and few tourists have ever visited. You will see national icons, including the Statue of Liberty and the Ellis Island Immigration Museum, and legendary neighborhoods, such as the Wall Street district and Greenwich Village (and view them all in very new ways). But you will also explore out-of-the way city parks, tiny beach communities, colonial houses, a working farm, industrial areas, neighborhood shopping centers, and small immigrant communities. And perhaps most remarkably, you will see some beautiful, unexpected views from the city's vast shore. We've planned these as tours of double discovery: discoveries through ancient time and modern space.

Unfortunately, we could not include all our favorite sites. Some had to be excluded on logistical or organizational grounds—they simply were not close enough to other sites to fit into a tour well. But we left out some sites for another reason. We know from bitter experience just how vulnerable archaeological sites are and how easily they and all the information they contain can be destroyed. Each site is unique, and once gone, it is gone forever. For that reason, and with great regret, we did not include sites that are subject to looting. Among these are the Staten Island sites, although one important exception can be seen in the distance from a stop on tour 1. All the sites that we include cannot be destroyed—they are protected because they are in well-populated, enclosed, or heavily patrolled areas, or they have been excavated and replaced by large buildings, or they are under protective layers of landfill or impenetrable streets.

We loved organizing these tours for you, and we hope that you love them too. Remember to put on your comfortable shoes, bring plenty of film and your sense of adventure, and be prepared to see a succession of New Yorks that you never knew existed.

Touring Gotham's Archaeological Past

New York Harbor

Tour 1

The Harbor Islands

This tour (fig. 1.1) is the only one that goes by boat. We planned it to be taken in conjunction with a visit to two of the nation's best-known attractions: the Statue of Liberty, on Liberty Island, and the Immigration Museum, on Ellis Island. These two islands are in the middle of New York's Upper Harbor. To their east is Governors Island, and bounding the southern margin of the harbor is Staten Island. The harbor itself, one of the finest in the world, has enormous historical significance. It was through here that Henry Hudson sailed on his famous voyage, a passage that led to the arrival of the first European colonists, and it was through here that millions of immigrants sailed on their way to start their new lives in the United States. The size and sheltered position of this splendid harbor helped New York become the nation's largest city and primary port, positions that it held for well over a century.

On this tour, you will see the harbor and its islands as they were thousands of years ago, when the harbor was dry land where mastodons roamed. You will learn about the first New Yorkers, discover thousand-year-old fishing and hunting camps, and see the burial places of those who once stayed on the islands. You will sail past the earliest-known remains of the city's Dutch settlement and visit some of the forts that protected the harbor. You will also see the final resting place of the ferry that carried thousands of immigrants on the last leg of their journey to the New World. Archaeologists working for the National Park Service (NPS) excavated many of these harbor sites.

Site 1. Castle Clinton

The tour begins at Castle Clinton National Monument in Battery Park in lower Manhattan. Take the 1 or 9 subway train to South Ferry, the 4 or 5 subway train to Bowling Green, or the N or R subway train to Whitehall Street, and walk south through Battery Park to Castle Clinton at the tip of Manhattan.

1

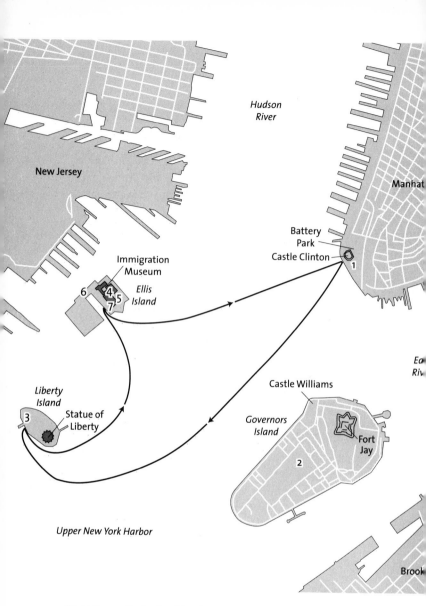

Fig. 1.1. Tour 1: the harbor islands

There you can buy tickets for the ferry to Liberty and Ellis Islands. The ferries operate on a loop, beginning at Battery Park, stopping first at Liberty Island and then at Ellis Island, and finally returning to Battery Park. For visiting hours and information on the islands, call 212-363-3200 or visit www.nps.gov/stli for Liberty Island and www.nps.gov/elis for Ellis Island; for information about ferry fees and schedules, call 212-269-5755 or visit www.statueoflibertyferry.com. While you are here, be sure to explore the old fort and see the exhibit on its history.

Designed by engineer Jonathan Williams, who also designed other fortifications of New York Harbor, Castle Clinton was built in 1808–11 to protect the city and guard access to the Hudson River. Although today it is located on Manhattan Island, it originally stood 200 feet off shore, in 35 feet of water, on an artificial island made just to support it—a remarkable engineering feat for its time. The fort, in effect a nonflammable "stable boat" made out of stone, was unsinkable. After it was decommissioned in 1823, it had a checkered history. First, the city turned it over to entrepreneurs who transformed it into Castle Garden, the popular entertainment center where P. T. Barnum presented Jenny Lind, the "Swedish Nightingale," in 1850. In 1855 the state took it over and turned it into its Immigrant Landing Depot, the predecessor to the federal Ellis Island Immigration Center. By 1870, the landfill expanding Battery Park had enveloped Castle Clinton, connecting it to the island of Manhattan. The depot closed in 1890 and was soon replaced by the new federal center at Ellis Island. In 1896 the old fort began a third life as the New York Aquarium. When Robert Moses, the New York City Parks Commissioner, closed the aquarium a half century later, he wanted to demolish the fort, which he described as a "large red wart." But the castle became a cause célèbre for the city's preservationists, who brought a lawsuit to save it. Finally, the State Supreme Court ruled that the building be spared. In 1950 the castle was transferred back to the federal government, which designated it a national monument and gave it to the NPS to restore and run.

Castle Clinton's first connection with archaeology begins elsewhere, at the corner of Greenwich and Dey Streets in lower Manhattan, where the World Trade Center once stood. There, in

FORTIFYING THE UPPER HARBOR

Beginning before the Revolutionary War and lasting well into the nineteenth century, New York Harbor was a vital part of the defense system that protected not only New York but also the East Coast against foreign invasion. Before the War of 1812, Lieutenant Colonel Jonathan Williams, first superintendent of West Point and one of the country's first professional military engineers (and Benjamin Franklin's great-nephew), designed a new set of fortifications to guard the harbor, the city, and the Hudson River. The fortifications were placed so that the first line of defense was at the Narrows, the passage into the Upper Harbor between Brooklyn and Staten Island. Any enemy ship that got through the Narrows would have to run the formidable gauntlet of the fortifications of the Upper Harbor, facing first the guns on Bedloe's (now Liberty) Island; then those on Governors and Ellis Islands; next those at the West Battery (today's Castle Clinton), then just off the tip of Manhattan Island; and finally those of the North Battery, at Hubert Street on the Hudson River shore. No enemy ship approaching New York City through the Upper Harbor would ever be more than a thousand yards from cannon shot. These fortifications were so formidable that during the War of 1812 the British never even attempted to enter New York Harbor, even though they captured Washington, D.C.

1916, construction workers excavating for a subway tunnel along the old Hudson River shore encountered the keel and ribs from what many believe to be the *Tijger,* a ship, captained by the Dutch explorer Adriaen Block, that had burned in the Hudson River in 1614 (fig. 1.2). Workers arranged for the eight feet of the ship that intruded into the tunnel to be removed and taken to the seals' pool in the aquarium at Castle Garden. The remains, immersed in water to preserve them, stayed there until the aquarium closed. The ship then went to the Museum of the City of New York, where it remains to this day.

In the 1950s and 1960s, several NPS archaeologists excavated at the fort as a prelude to its restoration. In 1963, one of them, William Hershey, took advantage of the fact that construction

Fig. 1.2. The remains of what may be the *Tijger*, before they were re-moved from the ground to make way for a subway station. (The dendritic lines are cracks in the glass plate from which this photograph was made.)

workers had removed much of the superstructure of the over-lying aquarium and explored a fairly wide area beneath it. He discovered that the fort where you are now standing was not built according to Williams's design. The foundation walls that he uncovered showed that the casemate (the chamber behind the openings where the guns were placed) was much shorter than originally planned: although Williams had designed a 28-foot-long casemate, Hershey saw that it was in fact only 18 feet long, with a flagstone walkway making up the 10-foot difference. But Hershey also discovered that supports for the casemate wall had been built as if the original plan, with its 28-foot casemate, were going to be constructed. It looked as though the builders' decision to shorten the casemate had been made *after* the infrastructure to support the original case-mate had already been put in place (fig. 1.3). The infrastructure must have been incredibly expensive and time-consuming to build, and he wondered why the plans had changed after that work was already completed. But he was never able to figure out why. Years later, William Griswold, another NPS archaeolo-gist, became absorbed in the problem and was able to solve it when he came across some letters about the building of the fort that an NPS historian had discovered.

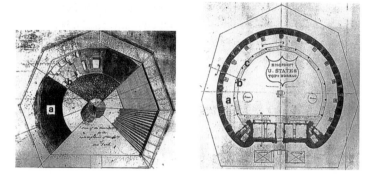

Fig. 1.3. The design for the construction of Castle Clinton, ca. 1810 (*left*), and a later plan of the fort as it was actually built, ca. 1820. In both illustrations, *a* indicates the casemate width and *b* the interior supports; *c* in the plan on the right indicates the flagstone sidewalk that was built to hide the design changes.

In reading the old correspondence, Griswold discovered that there had been problems with the fort's construction from the start. It was originally designed as a multi-tiered castle (or "casemated tower"), similar to Castle Williams at Governors Island (see site 2), to be built quite close to land, in only 15 or 20 feet of water. But city regulations required that it be placed 200 feet from shore, where the water was 35 feet deep. As a result, the fort's foundation had to be redesigned and made much more substantial than originally planned. As the project ran over budget and behind schedule, Secretary of War Henry Dearborn and later his successor, Williams Eustis, criticized Williams. They wanted the fort simplified to be just one tier tall. But Williams was adamant in wanting a second tier, so that the fort could accommodate 56 guns (instead of only 28) and quarters for enlisted men. Williams finally gave in and, discouraged, went back to West Point, leaving a subordinate in charge of completing the fort's single tier. But the excavations showed that much of the infrastructure for building a second tier had already been put in place, although many features had to be modified when the plans for the second tier were canceled.

Site 2. Governors Island

As the boat leaves Battery Park to cross the harbor toward Liberty Island, look at the island on your left. This is Governors

Island, by far the largest island in the Upper Harbor. The European colonists who first settled New Amsterdam called it Nutten Island, presumably because of the many nut trees that grew there, memorialized today only by the presence of a single walnut tree. In the early 1620s the Dutch West India Company set up a trading post and built a windmill there. In the 1690s the island was set aside for the use of the governor of the province of New York, and in the 1750s it was transferred to the military, which has used it almost continuously ever since. The army was there first, and in the 1960s the U.S. Coast Guard took it over. In 2003 the federal government transferred the island to the State of New York.

As you sail by, note the round, cheese-box-shaped sandstone structure on the island's northwest end. That is Castle Williams, named for its designer, Jonathan Williams, and built before the War of 1812. In the center of the island (and out of view) is Fort Jay, which was expanded and reconstructed from early fortifications built in 1755, during the French and Indian War.

In the 1980s and 1990s, archaeologists from the firms of Louis Berger and Associates and the Public Archaeology Laboratory, Inc. (PAL), worked on the island and discovered the remains of the long Native American and European presence there. While testing in an area of a golf course where construction workers were planning to dig a trench for an electric line, the Berger crew found the remains of a powder magazine that had been built before the War of 1812. Later, the Coast Guard called them back because workers excavating a trench through a parking lot had uncovered the graves of seven people. It turned out that the interred were probably all men and that their remains probably dated to the late eighteenth or early nineteenth centuries. They could have been British soldiers stationed on the island during the Revolutionary War or American soldiers held as prisoners of war there.

While carefully excavating the graves, the team noticed that the soil used to fill in several of the grave shafts had Native American artifacts in it, including Late Woodland pottery (dating from 1,000 to 400 years ago) and some stone flakes, debris left over from making stone tools. Evidently, when the graves were dug in the late eighteenth or early nineteenth centuries, they were placed in an area where there had once been a Late Woodland camp. In addition, near the burial area, also in disturbed soil, the Berger crew discovered a spear point that could date to the Late Archaic, around 4,000 years ago. So at least one hunter was probably hunting there thousands of years before the Late Woodland peoples stayed on the island.

More recently, when the U.S. Coast Guard was preparing to transfer ownership of the island, it had to follow federal law and identify important archaeological sites located there. As part of that effort, James Garman and Paul Russo led a team of PAL archaeologists in a study of the original part of the island —that is, the island as it had been before it was almost doubled in size by the addition of 79 acres of landfill in the early twentieth century. As they were exploring the eastern side, they made an amazing discovery. They gradually uncovered a circular stain, about 35 feet in diameter, which surrounded the remains of a series of squared-off wooden posts that had been stuck in the ground and that were also set in a circle (fig. 1.4). The posts had been carbonized, showing that they had burned. The team also found hand-wrought nails as well as debris from making stone tools in the soil that made up both the post holes and the stain. The nails' presence dated the posts to a time after the Europeans had arrived in New York.

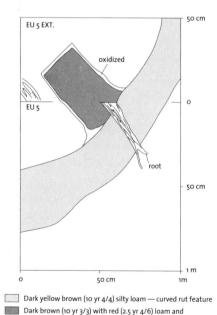

Fig. 1.4. An overview showing part of the curved stain and the rectangular post mold from the windmill on Governors Island

Dark yellow brown (10 yr 4/4) silty loam — curved rut feature

Dark brown (10 yr 3/3) with red (2.5 yr 4/6) loam and charcoal — burned post mold

Looking back at the history of the island, Garman and Russo realized that they could well have found the remains of the wind-powered sawmill that the Dutch West India Company had built there in 1625–26 and which the company continued to operate until at least 1639. By 1648, when the windmill was in ruins, the company ordered it dismantled or, if that was not possible, burned down, so that the iron from the structure could be salvaged. Iron was in short supply in the new colony and could not be wasted. The charred remains of the posts show that the decision had been to burn the sawmill.

When the archaeologists began to research Dutch windmills, they discovered that the wind-powered sawmill was invented in the 1590s (fig. 1.5). Looking at drawings of these mills, they realized that the post holes and the encircling curved stain that they discovered could well be from the smock that had housed the trestles on which the windmill sat. They sent some of the wood from one of the posts to be identified, and learned that it was from a white oak tree. They also arranged for radiocarbon dating on the same wooden sample. The results showed that the tree from which the post had been made had probably been cut down between 1570 and 1630—a time frame that fits the Dutch windmill well. All in all, these remains do appear to be from the Dutch West India Company's windmill and, as such, they represent the oldest Dutch remains that have ever been found in what is now New York City.

Near the windmill, the archaeologists discovered a Dutch glass trade bead (fig. 1.6). Beads like this have been found in up-

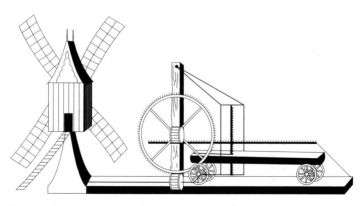

Fig. 1.5. A sixteenth-century wind-powered sawmill

Fig. 1.6. The glass trade bead found near the windmill on Governors Island

state New York, where most of the fur trade with the Native Americans took place, at sites that date to sometime before 1635. This bead is the sole possible piece of evidence for the trading post that the Dutch West India Company is reputed to have set up in the early 1620s. It is also one of very few items ever discovered in the city relating to those early years of contact between the Native peoples and the newcomers.

The PAL archaeologists also learned that the windmill had been built on top of another Native American Woodland site. Despite all the disturbance caused by the windmill's construction and more-recent activities, the archaeologists were able to identify what may have been two trash or storage pits and a number of artifacts, including twenty sherds from cooking or storage pots, from the earlier Indian settlement. They also located traces of a third Native American site, including some discarded sherds and other trash, in an area adjacent to one of the forts. These sites, astonishingly, survived all the construction that had gone on on the island. They are now protected from further disturbance.

Site 3. Liberty Island

Disembark at Liberty Island, home of the Statue of Liberty, one of the most famous American icons. As you visit the sites and enjoy the views of the harbor, bear in mind that the present park sits upon a rich buried past. On the west side of the island, archaeologists found traces of a thousand-year-old Native American site, which was overlain by a midden, or trash heap, dating to the late eighteenth or early nineteenth century.

In 1985, workers who were excavating a utility trench as part of the island's restoration discovered the site by digging right through it. With limited time and funding, NPS archaeologist Dick Hsu was able to explore the traces of this Native American shellfish-gathering station and hunting and fishing camp. He managed to sample part of the shell midden and excavate the contents of a large trash pit he discovered underneath it. The pit contained fish scales, bird bones, hickory nuts, charcoal, some pottery, and a spear point typical of Woodland times. Hsu had samples of the charcoal radiocarbon-dated; the dates averaged around 970 years ago, fitting in well with the date of the spear-point style. But because of lack of funding, he was not able to finish his analysis of the finds; he stored them carefully away.

Fourteen years later, another NPS archaeologist, William Griswold (who also worked on Castle Clinton; see site 1), returned to Liberty Island to study the site more extensively and to finish the analysis of the finds that Hsu had made. His work and that of his team of specialists tell us how this area used to look, why and when people came to the island, what they ate and used for fuel, and even what the climate was like a thousand years ago. In those distant centuries, perhaps even up to the time of the European arrivals, people came here to gather a variety of foods, some of which wound up in the trash pit or in the midden. The scientists identified the remains of oysters, soft-shell clams, mussels, turtles, white perch, oyster toadfish, and other fishes, as well as quail, canvasback, and other ducks. This variety suggests that Native peoples came to the island throughout the year to exploit its rich resources: the ducks that winter near the shore, the oyster toadfish that are more readily available in the summer, and the shellfish that are present year round. The charred hickory nuts mixed in with the bones and shells in the pit could have been used as fuel during a hunting foray, turned into beverages, or eaten on their own. They would have been plentiful in the fall and could have been gathered during duck-hunting or shellfishing forays.

While Dick Hsu was excavating the thousand-year-old Native American shell midden in 1985, he noticed that another midden lay on top of it. When Griswold went back to the site in 1999, he discovered that this more-recent midden was more extensive than first thought. Although it definitely dates to the late eighteenth or early nineteenth century, during the military phase of the island's history, no one knows exactly when the midden was formed or who made it. During the Revolutionary War, Tory refugees were housed on the island. Later, in reaction to British and French threats during the 1790s, first the state and then the federal government fortified the island, and in 1814 Fort Wood was completed. The fort continued in operation until the 1880s, when the Statue of Liberty opened with the eleven-pointed star-shaped fort incorporated into its pedestal.

Griswold believes that at least some of the midden had to

THE CHANGING ENVIRONMENT

Liberty Island's environment in Middle and Late Woodland times (2,000–400 B.P.) was radically different from its conditions today. In studying the bones from the midden, Tonya Largy, one of the scientists on Griswold's team, found those of a fledgling pelican, still too young to fly. Pelicans do not come to New York Harbor today; their breeding range extends only as far north as Maryland's coastal waters. The pelican's bones told her that it was much warmer here in Woodland times than it is today. Her interpretation is supported by her colleagues, botanists Lucinda McWeeney and David Perry, who noted that the radiocarbon dates from the trash pit coincide with the Little Climatic Warming Period (ca. 1,100–700 B.P.), when drought affected many local environments and cultures. Together, their results suggest that the climate was probably quite mild and perhaps quite dry when Native American peoples left their midden on Liberty Island.

McWeeney and Perry applied a new kind of analysis, one rarely used in archaeology, to the botanical finds here. They studied minuscule remaining tissues, known as parenchymatous tissues, of some of the plant materials found at the site. These come from any plant part other than wood, fruit, or seeds. But what the scientists saw in their microscopes raised more questions than answers. They found the tissues of water lily and flowering rush, both freshwater plants. Yet there is no record of a natural freshwater source on the island. So how did these freshwater plants arrive a thousand years ago on an island that today has no record of a natural freshwater source? And in addition to the question of how, there is also one of why. According to historical accounts, Native peoples roasted water lilies. But we don't know how the flowering rush was used. It may be that both plants were brought here from somewhere else, or it may be that the island once had a freshwater source that is now submerged.

The specialists also identified the small bits of charred wood that had been carefully excavated. They concluded that the modern, carefully manicured landscape was once very different, marked by hickory, oak, juniper, conifer, and elm trees.

have been formed by the soldiers stationed on the island in the late eighteenth or early nineteenth century, before the fort was finished. His reasoning is based on his discovery of a thick layer of sand overlying part of the midden, which he thinks came from the ditch that was dug around the fort. This scenario would indicate that the fort was built only after the formation of at least part of the modern trash heap. But team member Tonya Largy and other specialists who looked at the animal bones think that the midden must have been formed later on, in the early nineteenth century, after the fort was built. This is the only way they can explain the absence of oyster shells and rabbit bones from the trash. After all, in colonial times both oysters and rabbits were plentiful in the area. The island was often called Oyster Island, and in 1753 a real estate advertisement described the island as "abound[ing] with English Rabbits." The lack of the remains of both these animals suggests to the bone specialists that the midden was formed only after the colonial period, after the fort was built.

Site 4. Ellis Island's Main Building

Continue on the ferry to Ellis Island. As you plan your visit to the Immigration Museum, be sure to save time for several archaeological stops as well. Archaeologists working at Ellis Island over the past twenty years have added new dimensions to any visit here. The first stop is the Main Building at Ellis Island.

In 1984, when renovations began on this building for the new Immigration Museum, archaeologists were involved in the work. Therefore, they were ready to act the following spring when construction workers excavating in the basement came upon fragments of human bone and Native American pottery in the disturbed soil surrounding the footing of one of the building's support columns. Nearby, the archaeologists saw signs of a shell midden, buried about three feet below the basement floor. That summer, archaeologists began testing under the basement floor, looking for more evidence of the Native American presence on the island. Their excavations confirmed the presence of a nearby midden and yielded shells, animal bones, and a few artifacts.

When the bones were first studied, they appeared to be from a non-European, nonagrarian, nonurban people. But it was important to everyone involved to know more precisely whose bones they were, and in 1986 physical anthropologist Jean DeRousseau of New York University conducted a more intensive analysis of them. She identified three individuals, two of whom she thought were female. Although the bones were fragmentary, she said that they could well be Indian because of observed dental traits: the lack of cavities and of overbite and the presence of heavy wear on the teeth. So even though radiocarbon dating of bone samples from two of the individuals was inconclusive and the bones had been found in soil that had been disturbed in the nineteenth century, Hsu argued that the full weight of all the evidence—an intact Native American shell midden in the immediate vicinity of the human remains; the physical characteristics, especially the dentition, noted by the anthropologists; and the absence of recorded European burials in the area—pointed strongly toward a Native American burial rather than an unrecorded modern European one.

These dramatic discoveries suggested that the Main Building, through which millions of immigrants had passed as they entered America looking for a new life, was built on top of a Native American site. The discoveries of the bones and the adjacent midden lying beneath this shrine to American immigration took on great symbolic value for the descendants of the Native peoples who were living here at the time of the European incursions. Representatives of the Delaware Indians, many of whom live in Canada and Oklahoma today, have been actively involved in making decisions about the analysis of the bones and their ultimate disposition (fig. 1.7).

Fig. 1.7. Delaware spiritual leaders from Oklahoma and Canada gathered at Ellis Island in 1987 for a blessing ceremony honoring the remains of their ancestors recovered during renovations of the Great Hall of the Immigration Museum

THE DELAWARE BLESS THE BONES

On several occasions, representatives of the Delaware Indians returned from Oklahoma and Canada to their ancestral homeland, Lenapehoking, of which Ellis Island is a part, to bless the human remains found there. Before the analysis of the bones was begun in 1986, the NPS arranged for the bones to be sanctified by Linda Poolaw, then vice president of the Delaware Tribe of Western Oklahoma and representing three branches of the Delaware diaspora. On her flight to New York, Poolaw described what her mission meant to her as a Delaware: "Way above the clouds, looking down on the ground I was trying to imagine my ancestors crossing over all that land from the East Coast. How difficult it must have been."

At the laboratory where the analysis was to take place, Poolaw "smoked" the bones, using cedar brought from her home. Then all the participants, including the physical anthropologist, the NPS officials, and the Native Americans, "ran" smoke over themselves to purify themselves and restore spiritual balance. Following the ceremony, the study of the bones began. Some Delaware were concerned that the ceremonies for reburying the bones be conducted in the Delaware language, so that they would be familiar to the ancestors. Because some of the Delaware-speakers and ritual leaders were advanced in years, a consecration ceremony was held a year later, with the idea that there would be a formal reburial at a later date. Representatives from three branches of the Delaware and from the NPS were present at this ceremony, which was held on Ellis Island. Delaware "prayer-givers" wrapped fragments of the bones in deerskin to represent each of the individuals being blessed, placed tobacco and corn in the bundle, and painted it. Then the oldest Delaware from each group led the other representatives to the part of the island that faces Manhattan. They apologized to their ancestors for disturbing their rest and promised a proper reburial. This public prayer was followed by private prayers and rituals. Describing the ceremony to a reporter, Edward Thompson, aged 83, said, "We're preparing [the ancestors] to live forever and ever in tranquility." The bones were reburied in a third ceremony in 2003.

These ancestral bones, along with others since found, were reburied on Ellis Island in May 2003. Representatives of various Delaware groups from the United States and Canada took part in the ceremony. Publicly recognizing an early Delaware presence in this area and doing so at Ellis Island, the national symbol of subsequent European immigration, has enormous symbolic significance for Native peoples and other Americans, as well as for overseas visitors. The monument marking the reburial spot is a highly charged symbol of a new kind of American history, one in which both the ancient and the modern occupants are acknowledged as sharing a common ground, with their histories firmly joined. The monument is on the eastern edge of the island, near the exhibit on Fort Gibson, our next site.

Site 5. Ellis Island's Wall of Honor

The next archaeological stop is an open-air exhibit at the Wall of Honor, behind the Main Building, to the left of the door leading outside from the cafeteria. The display is in two parts, both outside and inside the circular wall.

Archaeologist Richard Hunter directed excavations here in 1992 just before the installation of the Wall of Honor. Before digging, the Hunter team studied the history of the island and learned that Ellis was originally the smallest of the harbor islands and that in its early history it was used as a base for shad fishing and oystering. The government began to fortify the island in the 1790s, building Fort Gibson, which had its battery on the southeastern part of the island, where you are standing (fig. 1.8). The military continued to control the island until 1890, and the federal government opened the immigration station here in 1892. After the original wooden immigration station burned in 1897, the government rebuilt it as the limestone and brick fireproof structure you see today, which opened in 1900. Designed to accommodate as many as a half-million immigrants annually, the building soon proved too small when the numbers of immigrants sometimes swelled to almost a million a year. The government then used landfill to enlarge the island (today it is nine times its original size) and ultimately built 33 additional buildings. It is estimated that by the time the U.S. consulates took over immigration inspection in 1924, approximately 12 million immigrants had passed through the island. Between 1924 and 1954, when the facility finally closed, the island was used as a deportation center, a Coast Guard station, and, during World War II, an internment camp for Japanese, Italian, and German aliens.

Before they went into the field, the Hunter team superimposed old maps of the island on top of each other, to see what they might find when they started digging. Because of their research, they were not surprised when they uncovered the remains of part of Fort Gibson, including parts of its exterior wall (which also formed the sea wall upon which its gun emplacements were built) and the buttresses that supported it, and a section of the concrete floor from the old Disinfecting House that had been part of the original immigration center, the one that had burned down in 1897. What did surprise them, however, was how superbly these remains had been preserved.

Hunter, realizing the importance of these finds, directed his crew to open up a wider area and see how much was left. He then alerted local archaeologists to what he had found. Together, he and the archaeological community were successful in making the Ellis Island Foundation and the NPS aware of the significance of the finds so that they were preserved intact and

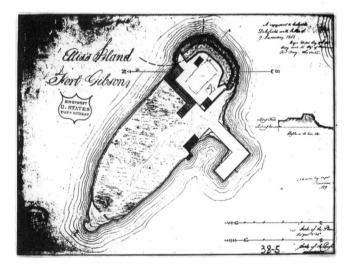

Fig. 1.8. A plan of Fort Gibson, Ellis Island, "drawn by Capt. Poussin, 1819." Note the battery at the southeastern end of the island and the dashed semicircle, which indicates the location of the Wall of Honor.

ultimately turned into the exhibit that you see here today. The remains of Fort Gibson are well explained in the exhibit text. Not mentioned in the text is a fragment of concrete floor from the Disinfecting House of the first immigration center, which is included in the display inside the wall.

Site 6. The Old Ferry Slip at Ellis Island

When you have finished visiting the museum, walk over to the old wooden ferry slip and art deco ferry building at the head of the modern slip where today's ferries tie up.

This ferry building was built in the 1930s, as part of a Works Progress Administration project. Beneath the water in the wooden slip are the remains of the ferry *Ellis Island*. The boat had been put into service in 1904, and it continued as the only regular ferry connecting Ellis Island with Manhattan for half a century, until the immigration center closed in 1954. In other words, the ferry had transported almost all of the 12 million immigrants who passed through the island on the way to their new lives (fig. 1.9).

After the immigration facility closed, the ferry was left docked in the slip. Fourteen years later, in 1968, the boat sank. When the NPS hired divers to investigate the ferry soon after, they discovered that it was resting on its side at an angle of about seven degrees, with three-quarters of its hull submerged in mud. The NPS personnel recommended that the ship be recorded with measured drawings and photos before it disintegrated. As the restoration of Ellis Island was planned, however, documenting the ferry was put on the back burner. Finally, in 2002, NPS archaeologists who specialize in underwater work began the project of documenting the *Ellis Island*. Diving down

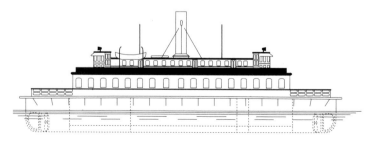

Fig. 1.9. A schematic drawing of the ferry *Ellis Island*

Fig. 1.10. Matt Russell, an NPS archaeologist, recording the hull of the sunken ferry *Ellis Island*. The object to the right of the diver is a fuel tank vent.

into the slip, where visibility was limited to just a few feet, archaeologists from the NPS Submerged Resources Center recorded the structure of the *Ellis Island* just as historical architects working on dry land might record the structure of a standing building (fig. 1.10). They confirmed that the ferry is deteriorating, and based on their report, the NPS will have to decide whether to let it continue to deteriorate or to try to raise and rehabilitate some of it. Although relieved that the ferry has at least been documented, many think that efforts should be made to save it, because the ferry ride on the *Ellis Island* from the island to the Battery was the final leg of the immigrants' journey. Ellis Island, after all, was not their destination. It was only after they had stepped off the ferry in Manhattan that they had at last reached their new home in the United States.

Site 7. The Harbor and Staten Island, as Seen from Ellis Island

As you wait for the ferry to bring you back to Manhattan, enjoy the spectacular view of the harbor and notice particularly Staten Island, to the south, behind the Statue of Liberty and just to the right of the Verrazano Narrows Bridge. This large suspension bridge connects Staten Island and Brooklyn. So far in our harbor tour, we have been examining the archaeological sites left by the Native Americans and Europeans who lived here after the landscape took on its roughly modern form, around 4,000 years ago. But before that time, this landscape was dramatically different. Twenty-one thousand years ago, at the height of the last Ice Age, the land that is now New York was uninhabitable, most of it covered by tons of glacial ice that was in some places more than 9,000 feet thick. The ice sheet extended as far south as today's Long Island and Staten Island. Because sea levels were at least 300 feet lower than they are now, the Atlantic shore was more than a hundred miles to the east of its current location, and vast areas of the continental shelf that today are covered with water were dry land to the south and east of where you are now. By around 12,500 years ago, the glacier had retreated north and much of this area had become a marshy plain, dotted with ponds and bisected by the Hudson River. Hills and high ground marked the landscape, including portions of present-day Ellis and Liberty Islands, as well as Staten Island just across the harbor.

Gradually the marshy plain was replaced by a new landscape, one of pine and spruce forests with small stands of oaks. Large animals, such as mastodon, roamed across the area, as did smaller ones like caribou, moose, elk, and even rabbit. This is the landscape that the first New Yorkers, a people archaeologists call Paleoindians, saw when they arrived here 11,000 years ago. In the millennia that followed, the sea level rose, gradually drowning the exposed land. But for thousands of years, when people were first living in the New York area, Ellis, Liberty, and Governors were not islands but hillocks rising above the plain, perhaps surrounded by marshland. The area was landlocked; the Atlantic shore was almost a hundred miles to the

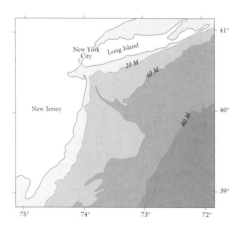

Fig. 1.11. The modern shoreline and the relative position of the shorelines approximately 6,000, 8,000, and 11,000 years ago, when the shoreline was lower than it is today by 20, 40, and 80 meters, respectively

east (fig. 1.11). So 11,000 years ago you could have simply walked from here, "Ellis Hill," over to "Liberty Hill," and then on over to the high ground of Staten Island.

One of the rare Paleoindian sites known in the East was discovered on Staten Island along the industrial waterfront of the Arthur Kill. In Paleoindian times the kill, today a great marine waterway separating Staten Island from New Jersey, was just a small brackish stream. Parts of the western shores of Staten Island that now stand about 9 feet above the kill rose about 75 feet above that stream when Paleoindians lived there.

Fig. 1.12. A fluted point from Staten Island. The base of the point is thinned by removing a channel, or "flute," from each side. The flute runs up the midline of the spear point and gives it its name.

A team of local avocational archaeologists discovered this important site in the 1950s. The group, which included Albert Anderson, often went out after work and on weekends to look for artifacts, bringing their nephews and sons along with them. One day, when they were searching in an area near the Arthur Kill where a lot of construction work was going on, Anderson's young son spotted a distinctive Paleoindian spear point —a fluted Clovis point—that had been churned up by earthmoving equipment (fig. 1.12). Over the years they found other Paleoindian artifacts in the same area and nearby. All told, they found about 120 of these ancient artifacts. Knowing the importance of their finds, they notified Herbert Kraft of Seton Hall University, who, with their help, analyzed and wrote up the finds. And the finds are astonishing because of their age, rarity, and survival for 11,000 years in the torn-up waterfront of one of the largest cities in the world.

Because of the work of Kraft, Anderson, and his group, we now know that one of the things that the Paleoindians were doing at this site was getting equipment ready for a hunt. This was a lengthy business, as modern experiments have shown that each spear point can take several hours to make. At this Staten Island camp, the archaeologists found several points that had shattered while being made. We know that the hunters were also making spear shafts here because Anderson and his team found the stone tools—spokeshaves and scrapers— that the hunters used to trim and prepare the wood for them.

THE PEOPLING OF THE AMERICAS

Most archaeologists believe that sometime during the last Ice Age, small family groups of peoples, perhaps arriving in several waves, entered and colonized the Americas. Many think that these first Americans arrived by crossing the Bering Strait from Siberia into Alaska and then made their way down to the interior of the Americas. But there is no consensus on exactly where or when they first arrived on the continent. Although probably not the first people in what is now the United States, the earliest populations for whom archaeologists have found widespread evidence across the continent are a group they refer to as Paleoindians. The earliest Paleoindians, called the Clovis people, were here about 11,000 years ago. Paleoindians were a mobile people with a small population. Their sites were relatively small and few in number, and not many have survived the enormous natural and cultural disturbances to the landscape over the past 11,000 years. Many of their encampments in the East may have been built way out on the exposed continental shelf, closer to the early shoreline. In fact, those coastal areas may have been far more attractive to these pioneering peoples than the inland area that New York was in those days. This makes it all the more astonishing that one of the few places that can attest to that great human undertaking, the exploration and settlement of North America, was found in the modern urban sprawl of New York City.

Although it is tempting to picture these hunters, armed only with spears fitted with Clovis points, stalking a mastodon across land that is now New York Harbor or even on the hills that are now Ellis and Liberty Islands, it is highly unlikely that such a dramatic encounter ever took place. Although mastodon remains have been found throughout the East (even in peat deposits in the Harlem River and upper Manhattan), none have ever been found in association with any Paleoindian artifacts. There is no evidence that Paleoindians anywhere in the East depended on these massive animals as a staple in their diet and focused their lives around hunting them. The evidence from

Fig. 1.13. A drawing of a reconstructed Paleoindian settlement in the Northeast. The pioneering Paleoindians, the first New Yorkers, may have lived in similar homes here.

other sites suggests that these early peoples hunted smaller, more readily available game, such as caribou, fox, marten, or hare. They also fished and gathered a variety of such plant foods as hawthorn plums, ground cherries, grapes, and seeds. But these first New Yorkers were doing far more here than just getting food. All kinds of tools were found: wood- and hide-working tools, knives, drills, and even gravers for working on bone and antler. This wide range of tools suggests that small family groups came here and stayed for a while before moving on (fig 1.13). The women may have used the scrapers to transform the hides brought in from a successful hunt into the boots and clothes that every family member needed for survival, or into the bedding and tent covers that were equally necessary in these post-glacial years.

These first peoples stayed in a New York that today we can barely imagine. We don't know their names, how they dressed, or what they called this land. But we know they were here. They were the first to see, name, and claim this land we now call New York. Their story is the opening chapter in the city's long and dramatic history.

Return on the ferry to Battery Park in Manhattan, where you can catch the 1 or 9 subway at South Ferry, the 4 or 5 subway at Bowling Green, or the N or the R subway at Whitehall Street.

Tour 2

Lower Manhattan Dutch New Amsterdam, Colonial New York,
and the Premier City of the New Nation

This tour leads you through lower Manhattan, from the canyons of Wall Street through the historic buildings at the South Street Seaport to the government buildings of City Hall Park and Foley Square (fig. 2.1). This is the old city, the part that was once Dutch New Amsterdam and early New York.

When the Dutch West India Company founded the settlement of New Amsterdam in Munsee territory in 1624–25, they centered it around Fort Amsterdam, strategically located at the foot of Manhattan Island. From there the company could protect the Hudson River and keep its own fur trade with the Native Americans safe from European competitors. And the settlers also had access to one of the finest natural harbors in the world, where they could switch the furs from riverboats to oceangoing ships for the transatlantic voyage.

Within a year of their arrival, the company began to import enslaved Africans to help meet its needs for labor, thus beginning the cruel tradition of slavery in New York that was to last for 200 years. It also embarked on wars with the Indians, particularly in the 1640s and 1650s; by the end of the century most Native Americans had left the city. The English conquered the Dutch colony in 1664, changed its name to New York, and with one short interruption, held it for more than a century. After the Revolutionary War, the city, which had been only the third largest in the British colony, became the premier metropolis of the new nation and attracted immigrants from all over Europe.

Since the 1970s, professional archaeologists have excavated more than a dozen sites here in lower Manhattan. They have recorded the lives of Dutch and English colonists, enslaved Africans, and the many immigrants who flocked to the burgeoning nineteenth-century metropolis.

Pearl Street, looking south. In the seventeenth century, Pearl Street was the East River shore. The buildings on the left are built on landfill, and the sidewalk on the right is on fast land.

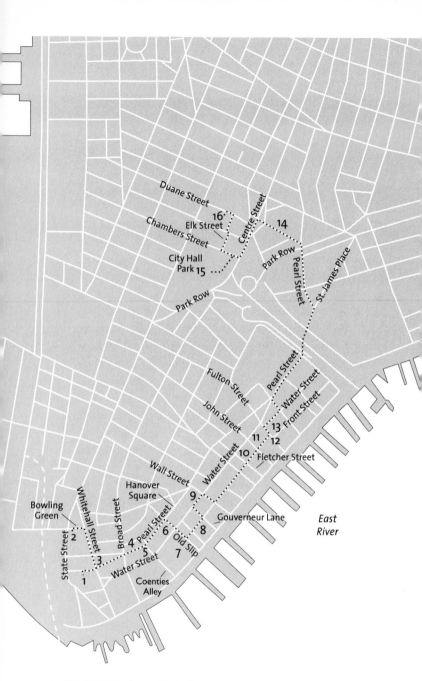

Duane Street

16
Elk Street
Chambers Street

Centre Street

14

City Hall
Park 15

Park Row

Pearl Street

St. James Place

Park Row

Fulton Street

Pearl Street

John Street

Water Street
Front Street

13

11 12

Water Street

10 Fletcher Street

Wall Street

Hanover
Square

9

Bowling
Green

Whitehall Street

Broad Street

Pearl Street

6

Gouverneur Lane

East
River

State Street

2

4

8

3

5 Old Slip

Water Street

7

Coenties
Alley

1

Fig. 2.1. Tour 2: lower Manhattan

Site 1. 17 State Street: New York Unearthed

Several subway trains lead to the first stop on the tour: take
the 1 or the 9 to South Ferry, the N or the R to Whitehall Street,
or the 4 or the 5 to Bowling Green. Seventeen State Street is a
curved steel office tower just opposite Battery Park. New York
Unearthed, the urban archaeology center run by the South
Street Seaport Museum, is located in a small building in the
plaza. For hours, call 212-748-6248 or visit www.southstseaport.
org/archaeology/nyunearthed.html; admission is free.

This small archaeological museum is the result of a cause
célèbre for preservationists and archaeologists. The story
began in 1985, when the William Kaufman Organization began
preparations for building the 42-story office tower with the
spectacular harbor views that you see here today. When the developer applied for a zoning variance, the project underwent
environmental review, and the city's Landmarks Preservation
Commission flagged the site for archaeological study because it
was located in the heart of New Amsterdam. In early 1986 the
developer hired archaeologist Joan Geismar to begin the background study. But at the same time, and for reasons that are
still disputed to this day, the developer received a permit to dig
for the foundation of an "as-of-right" building, which required
no environmental review at all. Bulldozers proceeded to excavate for the foundation, destroying any archaeological site that
might have been there.

Archaeologists and preservationists were alarmed not only
because a potential archaeological site had been destroyed but
also because the review process itself was threatened. If this
developer got away with violating an established process, why
would any developer ever comply? The Landmarks Preservation
Commission proposed that the developer receive its zoning
variance only if it agreed to create and maintain a small museum of New York City archaeology at the site. After a great
deal of wrangling, the developer agreed. In the *New York Times*
on May 6, 1990, the developer, Melvyn Kaufman, was quoted as
saying, " We were punished, so to speak. . . . The city made all
kinds of terrible threats. I said: 'What do you want us to do? I
can't put it back. You want to shoot me? Shoot me.'" In 1990
Kaufman established New York Unearthed, New York's first (and

only) museum devoted to its archaeological heritage, as restitution to the people of the city for the destruction of a possible archaeological site. The exhibits are on two floors, at ground and basement levels. Here you will see artifacts from archaeological sites spanning the entire history of the city, from Native American times through the twentieth century.

Site 2. One Bowling Green: The National Museum of the American Indian

As you leave 17 State Street, turn right in the plaza and right again on Pearl Street, continuing to Whitehall Street. Turn left and walk two blocks up Whitehall to the corner of Bowling Green. There at One Bowling Green, on the site where Fort Amsterdam was located in the seventeenth century, is a large Beaux-Arts building, which was formerly the U.S. Customs House and is now a branch of the Smithsonian National Museum of the American Indian. On either side of the imposing staircase is a series of bronze plaques describing Native American New York. For the museum's hours and admission policy, call 212-514-3700 or visit www.nmai.si.edu. Go back to the corner of Whitehall and Pearl.

Site 3. Pearl and Whitehall Streets: The Broad Financial Center

Just across Whitehall, on the northwest corner of Pearl, is a building with a facade of dark glass. This is the Broad Financial Center. Continue alongside the building a third of the way up the block toward Broad Street.

On this block, Joel Grossman of Greenhouse Associates directed excavations in the winter of 1983–84, before the construction of the office tower you see here today, and discovered many traces of Dutch New Amsterdam's early days. The team uncovered part of a warehouse and household goods from several homes on the block (fig. 2.2).

At almost this very spot, the archaeologists discovered the foundation walls and stone cobble floor of the warehouse that Augustine Heermans built in the mid-seventeenth century. Heermans, a Bohemian born in Prague, was a merchant who dealt in Hudson River furs, Virginia tobacco, wines, and provisions. He was also active in the trade in enslaved Africans. The archaeologists found quantities of red roofing tile associated

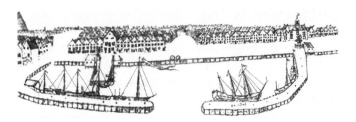

Fig. 2.2. A detail from the Labadist General View, by Jasper Dankaerts, showing the city ca. 1679. The Broad Financial Center now stands on the left half of the block that faces the small pier. The small house to the right of that pier had been built for Cornelis van Tienhoven. The large building with the cupola at the head of the right arm of the Great Dock is the State House; the King's House Tavern is to its right.

with the warehouse, suggesting that it was a substantial structure built in the Dutch style. They also discovered, wedged between the cobbles that paved the warehouse floor, a Dutch *jeton* or counter, used for calculating accounts (fig. 2.3).

In addition, the Grossman team uncovered several features from the backyards of Dutch households on the block. Two of them were located on land that Cornelis van Tienhoven owned in the mid-seventeenth century, just beyond Heermans's warehouse. Van Tienhoven, a native of Holland who arrived in New Amsterdam in the 1630s, served as the Dutch West India Company's secretary and held other offices as well. He was a controversial figure in the small colony and was known for his cruelty to his Indian neighbors. In fact, in 1656, the company fired him; it was said that there could not be peace with the Indians as long as he was in the colony. Later that year he disappeared. It still is not clear whether he absconded or committed suicide. But before he vanished, van Tienhoven had improved his Pearl Street parcel of land by tearing down the small house that had been on it when he bought it and building a larger one there. His wife continued to live in the new house until her death in 1663, and their son, Lucas van Tienhoven, a doctor, was still living there in 1679.

Fig. 2.3. Both sides of the counter or *jeton* found on the floor of Heermans's warehouse

One of the pits that the archaeologists found on this property was lined with barrels. Studying the artifacts inside it, the Grossman team reasoned that it had been filled in the 1650s. This was probably the pit from the privy that had been on the property when van Tienhoven first bought it and which he abandoned and filled in when he redeveloped the property two years later. The archaeologists found Dutch yellow brick and delft tiles in the privy (fig. 2.4), as well as some wooden beads and parts of a *roemer,* a Dutch hollow-stemmed goblet with a flared base. There were also a bone handle from a knife or fork and fragments of several Dutch-made tobacco pipes with their typical round "belly"-shaped bowls. Together, the artifacts from this privy make up the oldest collection of materials that we have from a home in Dutch New Amsterdam.

The second pit found on the van Tienhoven property, which archaeologists dated to the 1670s, when Lucas van Tienhoven was living in the house, was lined with a basket that had a wooden bottom with holes drilled through it. Based on its similarities to seventeenth-century features found in the Netherlands, the Grossman team thought that it originally was a drain. What is interesting about this drain, though, is what the excavators found inside it: one-half of a delft plate; some iron nails; pieces of window lead for holding window panes in place; a piece of lead shot; a needle and thimble; 17 stoneware marbles, some quite large; some quartzite flakes; three glass beads; and three shell beads, or pieces of wampum—the only pieces of wampum that have been found in lower Manhattan (fig. 2.5). Considered together, these objects do not seem like trash but rather like a cache of things that was carefully placed

Fig. 2.4. A delft tile from a privy on the van Tienhoven property. Ox-head motifs appear at the corners of the tile.

in the drain and left there, either purposely or by accident. Archaeologists have found caches with similar kinds of objects in underground "storage pits" in slave quarters in the plantation South. Although we will probably never know for sure, it is possible that an en-

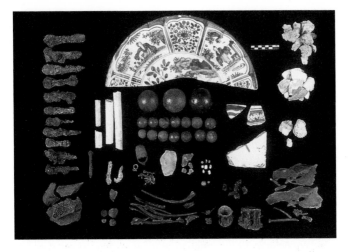

Fig. 2.5. The contents of the cache from the basket buried under the van Tienhoven house on Pearl Street in the 1670s

slaved African who lived in the van Tienhoven household placed these objects in the drain.

Site 4. Pearl Street near Coenties Alley: The Stadt Huys Block

Continue up Pearl Street and cross Broad Street; on the left is 85 Broad Street, the red conglomerate building that now houses the corporate headquarters of Goldman Sachs, the investment bankers. Continue toward the next corner, Coenties Alley, and stop when you reach the upright bronze plaque by the curb, commemorating the excavation of the Stadt Huys Block.

This block, where New Amsterdam's Stadt Huys or State House (and hence New York's first city hall) was located in the seventeenth century, is the site of the first large-scale archaeological excavation in New York City. The excavations here, which Nan Rothschild and Diana Wall directed in 1979–80 under the auspices of the New York City Landmarks Preservation Commission, were the test case which demonstrated that archaeologists could find important remains in one of the most urban parts of the world, the Wall Street district of Manhattan. They proved that the relatively shallow basements of the city's older buildings could protect and seal in archaeological sites rather than destroy them. Because of the success of the excavations

SLAVERY IN NEW YORK

Although many people tend to associate slavery only with the plantation economy of the South, slavery was widespread throughout the North as well. The Dutch West India Company began to import enslaved Africans in 1626, only a year after the founding of New Amsterdam. The English continued the practice to make up for the colony's perennial labor shortage. The colonists also enslaved Native Americans; most were sent to the West Indies. Later in the seventeenth century the enslavement of local Indians was banned, although members of other Native American groups continued to be held in bondage here until around 1740. But throughout its British colonial history, New York City's population of enslaved Africans was second in size only to that of Charleston, South Carolina. Finally, in the late 1790s, New York State began its slow and faltering steps toward emancipation, which was finally achieved on July 4, 1827, a relatively late date for a northern state.

The enslaved worked at a variety of jobs in New York. In the city, some were unskilled laborers, hired out by their owners to work on public-works projects or as stevedores at the city's docks. Others were highly skilled artisans who worked side by side with their owners, producing goods for market. Still others (especially women) labored in domestic service, performing the onerous tasks involved in running colonial urban households, or worked as vendors and peddlers in the city's streets and markets. In rural areas, enslaved women were household help and enslaved men, farm labor. Unlike in the plantation South, most of the enslaved men, women, and children of New York did not reside in separate quarters but instead lived under the same roofs as their owners. Some slept in cellars, others in garrets, and others still in "Negro kitchens" in their owners' backyards.

here, the city began to include the protection of archaeological sites in its environmental review process.

Although the archaeologists digging at the Stadt Huys Block did not find any traces of the Stadt Huys itself (they think that later development on the block destroyed the building's foundation), they did uncover part of the building next door, the Lovelace Tavern or King's House, which was built in 1670 and burned down in 1706 (see fig. 2.2). Inside the tavern's foundation walls they found thousands of pieces of white clay tobacco pipes, wine bottles, and wine glasses, attesting to the building's use as a tavern. As you walk around, note the paving stones outlining the Stadt Huys and the tavern, and the windows set into the sidewalk showing segments of the tavern's stone foundation wall.

Site 5. Pearl Street and Coenties Slip

Walk to the corner of Pearl Street and Coenties Alley and look up and down Pearl Street.

During the seventeenth century, Pearl Street was perched along Manhattan's East River shore—in fact, people say the street's name came from the mother-of-pearl oyster shells discarded along the beach here. All the land to your right, between Pearl Street and the East River (today three blocks to the east), is landfill and was part of the river when the Dutch first arrived. Archaeologists have excavated sites located on the original island of Manhattan (including the Broad Financial Center and Stadt Huys Block sites) and sites on the landfill.

Landfilling, or making land, has been extremely important in the growth of New York City. More than a third of lower Manhattan is composed of "made land." And "making" city real estate is a very old practice, which the colonists introduced into the city in the 1650s. New Yorkers filled in the blocks between Pearl and Water Streets first, in the late seventeenth and early eighteenth centuries; those between Water and Front Streets in the mid-eighteenth century; and those between Front and South Streets, on today's East River shore, in the late eighteenth and early nineteenth centuries. Archaeologists digging in the landfill have discovered a lot about the landfill process, including how the first city developers held the landfill in place and how they built on it so that their buildings did not crack as the landfill settled beneath them.

Site 6. Pearl Street and Old Slip: 7 Hanover Square

Walk north along Pearl Street for one block to Hanover Square. On the right is 7 Hanover Square, the large red brick building with granite trim.

Fig. 2.6. The seventeenth-century stone walls at the 7 Hanover Square site. The Livingston House, which takes up two lots, is in the lower-left corner of the view; the Dutch houses are the smaller ones toward the top of the view.

Here, in 1981, before the building was built, Nan Rothschild, Arnold Pickman, and Diana Wall led the first large-scale excavation of a New York City landfill block. The team discovered a lost technique for building on landfill in New York when they uncovered the foundation walls of the first set of buildings erected on the block, built in the 1680s and 1690s (fig. 2.6). On this seventeenth-century landfill block, builders circumvented the problem of building on unsettled fill by laying the footings of the buildings' stone foundation walls directly on the beach and in the intertidal zone, and then placing the landfill around the walls. The load of the buildings therefore rested on natural soil and not on the landfill, so the settling of the landfill could not undermine the buildings. Because of this engineering technique, the archaeologists were able to find the walls well preserved under the basements of later buildings.

The stone walls showed the archaeologists that what you now see as a modern office tower was a seventeenth-century block lined with many houses built in different styles: the home of the British Livingston family was built in the fashionable British style, with its broad side facing the street, while the homes of the Livingstons' ethnically Dutch neighbors were much smaller and built in the Dutch style, with their gable ends facing the street.

Site 7. Old Slip and Water Street: Cruger's Wharf

Walk east on Hanover Square, which becomes Old Slip, to Water Street, and look across the street at 55 Water Street, the long gray building to the south of the slip. In the eighteenth century, this was the site of Cruger's Wharf.

While construction workers were digging for the building's foundation in 1969, Paul Huey and a small crew sponsored by the New York State Historic Trust had a brief opportunity to record part of Cruger's Wharf and some of the old layers of soil from both the old river bottom and the eighteenth-century landfill. This was the first chance that archaeologists had had to study the landfill and any of these waterfront structures. Cruger's Wharf extended out from the shore in an L-shaped configuration; it was later used to hold back the landfill that made up the block between Water and Front Streets (fig. 2.7).

As Huey notes, New York's waterfront was unusual in the Anglo-American colonies because it was made up of a series of slips, or block-long "canals," extending inland, instead of piers projecting out into the river. New Yorkers abandoned the slip system, a legacy of the city's Dutch heritage, only around the time of the Revolutionary War. Many of these old slips are immortalized in the names of the riverward ends of several streets in lower Manhattan, such as Coenties Slip, Old Slip, Burling Slip, and Peck Slip.

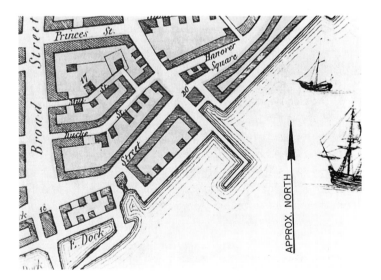

Fig. 2.7. A detail from Grim's plan of the city, showing the configuration of Cruger's Wharf in the early 1740s

Site 8. Gouverneur Lane and Front Street: The Assay Site

Walk farther east on Old Slip to Front Street, turn left, and stop at the corner of Gouverneur Lane; note the gray granite building on the east side of the street, One Financial Square (32 Old Slip).

In 1984, before this modern building was built, this was the Assay site, where archaeologists Roselle Henn and Diana Wall led an excavation. Later Charles LeeDecker and Terry Klein of Louis Berger and Associates analyzed the finds. The team discovered large wooden wharves that had been built here in the 1790s to hold back the landfill. All in all, the archaeologists were able to record more than a hundred linear feet of three different wharves, each of which measured more than fifteen feet in height (fig. 2.8). The construction techniques used to build the wharves were passed down through an oral tradition that was abandoned in the early nineteenth century. Because these techniques were not recorded in writing, the archaeological record is the only way to find out about many of them.

The reason that the archaeologists were able to study such a large portion of the wharves was that construction workers had completed a slurry wall around the site. The slurry wall (like the "bathtub" at the World Trade Center site) sealed the site so that groundwater could not seep in. It also allowed the archaeologists to explore the old river bottom, which had been

Fig. 2.8. The wharves that made up the seawall on the Assay site in the 1790s

covered by landfill around 1800. Unlike the discarded trash that archaeologists usually find, many of the artifacts on the river bottom had probably been lost by accident, dropped either overboard from a boat or off the side of the wharf that formed the 1790s shoreline. Many of the artifacts were made of metal, a material that archaeologists seldom find because in the past it was usually sold for scrap and recycled. The team found pewter plates and spoons, utensils that we know from estate inventories were ubiquitous in colonial homes but which are rarely found in the ground, as well as such personal items as shoe buckles, which probably fell off the shoes of passersby.

The archaeologists at the Assay site had another unprecedented opportunity: to recover direct evidence of the Great Fire of 1835. This fire, the most devastating ever to strike the city, destroyed almost seven hundred buildings in the area bounded by Coenties Slip, Wall and Broad Streets, and the East River. Archaeologists had often found a "fire layer" from this fire in their excavations in lower Manhattan, but usually it consisted of only a thin sheet of ash or charred wood. Here at the Assay site, however, they found a thick layer of burned material on top of a charred wooden basement floor. The layer contained the lower parts of the barrels, baskets, and crates filled with coffee beans, peppercorns, grapes, and Bordeaux wines that a grocer named Anthony Winans had stored in his basement at the time the fire struck (fig. 2.10). The charring from the fire helped preserve the organic material and kept it from decomposing during the intervening century and a half. The archaeologists learned from historical records that the fire did not wipe Winans out completely. By the next year, with typical New York resilience, he had reopened his grocery business in this same neighborhood.

Site 9. Wall and Water Streets

Turn left on Gouverneur Lane and walk back to Water Street, turn right, and proceed north to Wall Street. There on the west side of Water Street is the red brick and granite building at 75 Wall Street, the headquarters of Barclays Bank.

In 1984, Bertram Herbert and Terry Klein of Louis Berger and Associates directed excavations on this late seventeenth-century landfill block. They found a large number of artifacts

THE SPOON ON THE RIVER BOTTOM

One of the metal artifacts that the archaeologists found on the river bottom at the Assay site may have been placed there intentionally. They uncovered a spoon with several x's or +'s scratched on the inside of its bowl (fig. 2.9). In 1984, when the find was made, the archaeologists noticed the +'s but assumed that they had been scratched there accidentally. Years later, however, Diana Wall read a book by Leland Ferguson, an archaeologist who works in the South, which suggested another interpretation. In his book Uncommon Ground, *Ferguson noted the presence of incised +'s on the bases of some hand-built unglazed red earthenware ("colonoware") bowls from the Carolina low country. He argued that the +'s were "cosmograms" derived from the Bakongo people who live in today's Angola and Congo in West Africa, one of the places where the enslaved who were brought to North America were captured. The Bakongo use this cosmogram to depict the relationship between the earth and the water, and the living and the dead: the horizontal line represents the water that serves as the boundary between the living and their ancestors, while the vertical line represents the path of power across the boundary, from below (the land of the ancestors) to above (the land of the living). Ferguson maintained that the bowls were used as containers for sacred medicines ("minkisi"). Most of the marked colonoware bowls were discovered on the bottoms of rivers and streams, supporting the interpretation that the enslaved used them in rituals involving the water. So far, these bowls have not been found in the North. But when Wall read Ferguson's study, she remembered the spoon from the Assay site with the +'s incised on its bowl.*

The discovery of this spoon in the context of the river bottom suggests that some of the enslaved Africans in New York may have practiced a similar ritual here. If so, the evidence of that ritual was preserved for almost two centuries by the protective layer of landfill above it.

Fig. 2.9. The bowl of the spoon with the incised +'s that was found under the landfill on the river bottom at the Assay site

Fig. 2.10. A crate of bottles that had been stored on the Winans' basement floor

from many of the homes and businesses that stood here in the late eighteenth and early nineteenth centuries (fig. 2.11). The archaeologists found plates and crucibles from the home and workshop of silversmith Daniel Van Voorhis, who lived there in the 1780s (fig. 2.12); medicine bottles, jars (including one marked as a remedy for baldness—see fig. 2.12), and even a glass nipple shield for nursing mothers from the pharma-

Fig. 2.11. The corner of Wall and Water Streets, painted from the corner of the Barclays Bank site by Francis Guy, ca. 1797

Fig. 2.12. Some artifacts from the 7 Hanover Square site: (*left*) crucibles from the Van Voorhis silver shop, 1780s, and (*right*) an ointment pot (advertising a cure for baldness) from the Posts' apothecary shop, 1790s

ceutical shop that the brothers Joel and Jotham Post ran in the 1790s; and brown stoneware beer bottles from the 1820s counting-house of David Dunham, the auctioneer who was the first to use a steamship—the *Robert Fulton*—for the coastal run from New York to New Orleans and who died when the boom of a Hudson River sloop knocked him overboard.

Site 10. 175 Water Street: A Ship in the Landfill

Turn right and walk back down Wall Street to Front Street. Turn left and continue north on the west side of the street for two and a half blocks, crossing Fletcher Street, and stop in the middle of the block.

You are now standing alongside the spot where in 1981 archaeologists found the remains of an early eighteenth-century merchant ship in the landfill (fig. 2.13). Joan Geismar and nautical archaeologists Warren Riess and Sheli Smith led the excavations here, before the red granite and brick National Westminster Bank Building was constructed. Supporting the tenet that archaeologists make their best discoveries at the end of the field season, when it is often too late to excavate them, Geismar's team found the ship in the last week of the dig, after they had uncovered literally tons of artifacts from the homes and workshops that had been located here in the late eighteenth and early nineteenth centuries. Fortunately, the team was granted a 34-day extension to excavate the ship while construction began on other parts of the site.

Sometime between 1749 and 1755, laborers stripped the ship of all its fittings and hauled it out to become part of a bulkhead chain positioned to hold the new landfill in place when the block was filled. They filled the hull with a ballast of sand, cobbles, and yellow brick clinkers, and the ship was sunk in place. The archaeologists recorded the ship in measured drawings and photographs (fig. 2.14) and then removed the bow (which is now in the Maritime Museum in Newport News, Virginia, although there is talk of returning it to New York for exhibition at the South Street Seaport Museum). Construction workers took the rest of the ship from the site and dumped it unceremoniously in the modern-day Fresh Kills landfill on Staten Island.

Archaeologists who studied the ship's wood and the techniques used to construct it believe that it was built by English-trained shipwrights in the Chesapeake Bay area. They also discovered holes in the hull that had been drilled by teredo ship worms, which are native to the Caribbean. The holes show that the ship was active in the trade with the British West Indies, which was extremely important to the economy of eighteenth-century New York.

Site 11. 199 Water Street

Continue north on Front Street, cross John Street, and stop at 199 Water Street, the dark-gray granite home of Prudential

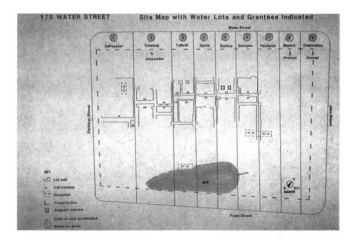

Fig. 2.13. A map of the 175 Water Street site, showing the lots, the names of their owners, and the location of the ship that was sunk to hold the landfill in place

Fig. 2.14. Archaeologists recording the structure of the ship discovered at 175 Water Street

Bache and the site of the Telco Block.

Diana Wall, Wendy Harris, and Jed Levin led excavations here in 1981, before the modern office tower covered this block, the site of many countinghouses and warehouses in the nineteenth and early twentieth centuries. The archaeologists discovered one cause of the dire health problems that plagued New Yorkers before the installation of piped water, sewers, and indoor plumbing in the nineteenth century: in the backyards behind the buildings on the block, they found brick cisterns, used for holding drinking water, right next to stone privy pits from outhouses (fig. 2.15). Seeing these utilities so close to each other underscored how easily drinking water could become contaminated by privy effluvia, contributing to the cholera epi-

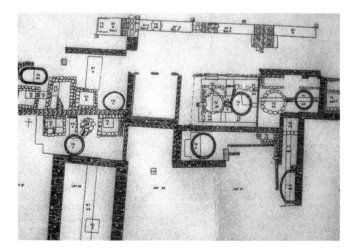

Fig. 2.15. A detail from a map of the Telco Block site, showing the narrow backyards with cisterns and privies placed side by side

demics that repeatedly swept through the city in the nineteenth century.

Site 12. Fulton and Front Streets: The South Street Seaport Museum

Continue up Front Street to Fulton Street. You are now in the
heart of the South Street Seaport Historic District. Be sure not
to miss the South Street Seaport Museum, which interprets
the history of the port of New York. It holds the world's largest
collection of artifacts from archaeological sites in New York
City and regularly incorporates them into its exhibits. For its
hours and admission policy, call 212-748-8600 or visit www.
southstseaport.org.

Site 13. 207 and 209 Water Street: Another Ship in the Landfill

Walk a short block west on Fulton Street to Water Street, turn
right, and proceed to 207 and 209 Water Street, the two Greek
Revival buildings with gray granite columns on the right, just a
few buildings north of the corner.

In 1978, when construction workers dug a sump in the basement of 209 Water Street to help drain the cellars on the block,
maritime historian Norman Brouwer, from the South Street
Seaport Museum, and archaeologist Robert Schuyler and his
students from the City University monitored the work. They
discovered an eighteenth-century ship buried in the landfill. It
was oriented east-west, perpendicular to the shore. Although
they could uncover only a nine-foot stretch of the ship (the rest
extended underneath the standing building), they could tell
that laborers had placed it there to help hold back the mid-
eighteenth century landfill, just as they had at 175 Water Street.

Two years later, when the South Street Seaport Museum
arranged for excavations to install a heating system in the
basement of the building next door at 207 Water Street, archaeologist Betsy Kearns, who was monitoring that work, was
not surprised when she discovered the other side of the hull
of the same ship. In both cases, the museum changed its construction plans in order to preserve the ship in the landfill. It
is still here under the foundations of these two buildings.

Site 14. 500 Pearl Street: The Notorious Five Points Slum

Walk a short block west to Pearl Street and turn right. Continue north, passing under the ramps leading to the Brooklyn Bridge. Go one block farther, to the corner where Pearl Street turns to the left (or west; the street you are on changes its name to St. James Place). Turn with Pearl Street, cross Park Row, and stop in front of 500 Pearl Street, the gray granite court building also called the Courthouse site. Edward Rutsch and Leonard Bianchi of Historic Conservation and Interpretation (HCI) led the excavations here in 1991, and Rebecca Yamin of John Milner Associates directed the analysis of the finds. This site gave archaeologists their first opportunity to explore the lives of the city's poor. Where you are standing was once the heart of the Five Points district, New York's most notorious nineteenth-century slum, immortalized by Martin Scorsese in his movie *Gangs of New York*. Middle-class New Yorkers demonized its mostly immigrant residents, and Charles Dickens described it as a place where "poverty, wretchedness, and vice, are rife" when he visited the neighborhood in 1842. But the plates, teacups, and other artifacts from the homes of the Italian, Irish, and German immigrants who lived on the site contribute to a new vision of the neighborhood. They show that the community that saw the birth of the modern working class was more stable than many scholars had thought: household goods similar to many of those found in the Five Points homes (fig. 2.16) were also found in the homes of their wealthier contemporaries in the city's middle-class neighborhoods. Unfortunately, most of the artifacts from this site were stored in 6 World

Fig. 2.16. Ceramics from the Courthouse site in the Five Points district

A NINETEENTH-CENTURY BROTHEL

*When Rebecca Yamin was analyzing the artifacts from the
Five Points site, she realized that one backyard privy contained items that were very different from those found elsewhere on the site: there were some very ornate ceramics, an
unusually high number of chamber pots, glass urinals designed for women (fig. 2.17), and a ceramic pot inscribed with
the words "AMAILLE, s.d. Vinaigrier." Yamin guessed that the
privy's contents had come from a brothel, and her subsequent
research showed that the building next to the privy had
housed a brothel in 1843, right around the time when the
artifacts had been thrown away.*

*In the nineteenth century, prostitution was the most lucra-
tive occupation open to a working-class woman. Most prostitutes came from working-class families in which one parent
had died or where there were problems at home. Although
many young women worked at prostitution full time, others
were "occasional prostitutes" who used prostitution to supple-
ment their incomes from other trades. Most left "the life" by
the time they were thirty or so and went on either to mar-
riage or to another profession. But some died young, from
venereal diseases, violence, or the complications of drug or alcohol addiction. Historians know a great deal about what
middle-class reformers thought about prostitution, but they
know little about it from the points of view of the women
who worked in the profession. Yamin's examination of the objects from the privy provided her with a new perspective that
highlighted the difference between the private lives of the
young women and their public lives at work.*

*The more ornate ceramics from the privy were the kind that
were commonly used in middle-class homes for entertaining;
in the brothels, they were probably used for serving the
middle-class male customers who would expect such ameni-
ties. There was an old-fashioned tea set made of Chinese export porcelain, punch cups, and wine bottles. The wine was
probably served in tumblers—there were 66 of them, but very
few wine glasses. The traces of food suggest that the brothel
served snacks like brandied fruits, olives or capers, veal, soft-*

shell clams, and coffee. None of these foods were found in other features at the Courthouse site. And archaeologists also found many personal items that the young women may have used in their public performance—perfume bottles, a miniature flask, combs, a hairbrush, mirror fragments, and the ribs from a folding fan.

Yet there were also poignant reminders of the private, dangerous side of prostitution. The three women's urinals presumably were used when the young women were sick in bed, perhaps from the venereal disease that was their occupational hazard (a contemporary study shows that almost half the prostitutes practicing in the city at mid-century suffered from syphilis). In addition to a syringe, there were medicine bottles, one—embossed BRISTOL'S EXTRACT OF SARSAPARILLA —prescribed specifically for venereal disease. But most tragic of all were the remains of three infants found in the privy.

Two of them were full term, and it is not known if they died of natural causes or were the victims of infanticide. The third, who had not reached term, had been aborted, either deliberately or spontaneously. But none of these infants had been buried; instead, their deaths had been hidden. All in all, Yamin's study presents a complex picture of the women of the brothel.

Fig. 2.17. Glass urinals from the privy behind the brothel at the Courthouse site

Trade Center and were destroyed in the terrorist attack of September 11, 2001.

Site 15. Chambers and Centre Streets: City Hall Park

Continue west on Pearl Street, cross Centre Street, turn left, and walk south. Cross Chambers Street to City Hall Park and walk toward the subway kiosk and the statue of Horace Greeley. Take a right into the park and continue down the path that separates the two large nineteenth-century buildings, the Tweed Courthouse (which fronts on Chambers Street) and City Hall (which faces south).

During the colonial period, this area was the city's Commons, a place at its northern edge where people could pasture their animals and where, as time went by, some of the activities that were considered better suited to the city's outskirts took place: the gallows was located here at the beginning of the eighteenth century, and later in the century the city put some of its public buildings here. By the end of the century, the Commons had been the site of two of the city's almshouses, three sets of barracks for housing British soldiers, and two jails, which during the Revolutionary War were used for housing American prisoners of war. Be sure to check for the footprints of some of these buildings, which are etched in bluestone in the park's paving.

This park has been the site of quite a few archaeological projects. In 1989 several archaeologists, including first Joel Grossman and then Sherene Baugher, directed excavations before the installation of a utility line running between the courthouse and City Hall. Where you are standing, they discovered the brownstone foundation and cellar hole of an eighteenth-century building. Inside the cellar they found architectural materials, remains of food, and other artifacts associated with this building, which may have served as the kitchen of the city's first almshouse (built in the 1730s), where food for the city's destitute was prepared. The artifacts included buttons made out of bone and "button blanks"—the flat pieces of bone (often the shoulder blades of cattle) from which the buttons were cut (fig. 2.18). The profusion of buttons and button blanks suggests that button making may have been one of the tasks that the city required of almshouse inmates in exchange for their support.

Petar Glumac of Parsons Brinckerhoff led another project here in 1998–99 in conjunction with the renovation of the park. Glumac's team excavated all over the northern part of the park, uncovering trash pits and the architectural remains of some of the eighteenth-century buildings, including the jail, located on the eastern side of the park. Some of the trash appears to have been associated with the almshouses, which were located where City Hall and the Tweed Courthouse are today, and some (including pieces from dozens of wine bottles)

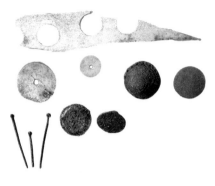

Fig. 2.18. Eighteenth-century pins, buttons, and a button blank for making bone buttons, from the city's almshouse

with the soldiers' barracks at the northern end of the park. And of course the Glumac team found coins and other things that people dropped as they walked through the park.

The Glumac project suffered from a problem that has plagued several of the archaeological projects in New York, including the Courthouse and Assay sites you have just visited (see sites 8 and 14). That is, there was no continuity between the team that excavated the site and the team that analyzed the finds. Glumac and his team performed the background research and all the field excavations for the project, but H. Arthur Bankoff, archaeological consultant to the Landmarks Preservation Commission and professor at Brooklyn College, and some of his colleagues are directing the ongoing analysis and interpretation of the finds, with help from graduate students at the City University. This sort of change of players usually stems from disputes about money; for example, after a project's excavations have run over budget, a developer may protest the cost of the analysis phase and negotiate a new contract with a new consulting firm or other entity. Unfortunately, a loss of archaeological information inevitably results.

A third project in the park, led by Carol Raemsch of Hartgen Archaeological Associates, was conducted as a prelude to the renovation of the Tweed Courthouse. Together, the Raemsch and Glumac teams uncovered more than fifty undisturbed burials here in the northern part of the park (as well as enormous piles of human bones in mass graves, which presumably came from burials that were disturbed during the construction of City Hall and the Tweed Courthouse in the nineteenth century). Whenever they uncovered an intact burial, the archaeologists followed the Landmarks Preservation Commission's policy, recording the fact that the burial was found and simply recovering it. As a result, we do not know whose burials were uncovered. Were they people from the almshouse? Soldiers stationed in the barracks? American or French prisoners of war? People executed at the gallows, including those who were hanged during the slave revolts of 1712 and 1742? People from the African Burial Ground, which might have extended into the park, further south than shown on maps? Or all of the above? Some archaeologists lament the fact that the identities of the burials remain unknown, but other people are pleased that the deceased, whoever they may be, are allowed to rest in peace.

Site 16. Elk and Duane Streets: The African Burial Ground

Walk back to the corner of Chambers and Centre Streets. Cross Chambers and walk west one short block to Elk Street. Take a right and walk two blocks north to the southwest corner of Elk and Duane Streets, the site of the African Burial Ground.

In 1991, archaeologist Edward Rutsch of HCI and his crew were working at this site, where the federal government was about to build the office tower that you see today at the next corner, 290 Broadway. They made the amazing discovery that the eighteenth-century "Negros Burial Ground" (fig. 2.19), which they knew had been located here but had assumed had already been destroyed by later building construction, had been preserved under a blanket of landfill 20 feet deep. The burial ground, which was in use for almost a century, originally extended from Broadway to Centre Street, encompassing about six acres. The burials were excavated at the site of the office tower at 290 Broadway; the grassy area at the corner of Elk and Duane Streets was originally part of the building site but is now being preserved to commemorate the cemetery.

Over the next year, Michael Parrington, working first for HCI and later for John Milner Associates, which took over the project, directed the team that excavated more than four hundred burials at the site, recovering the largest early burial population of people of African descent in North America. Anthropologist Michael Blakey of Howard University led the study of the site's human remains and has uncovered a wealth of information about the experience of enslaved Africans in colonial New York.

Historically, the African presence in early New York has been almost ignored. The little that we know about the lives of en-

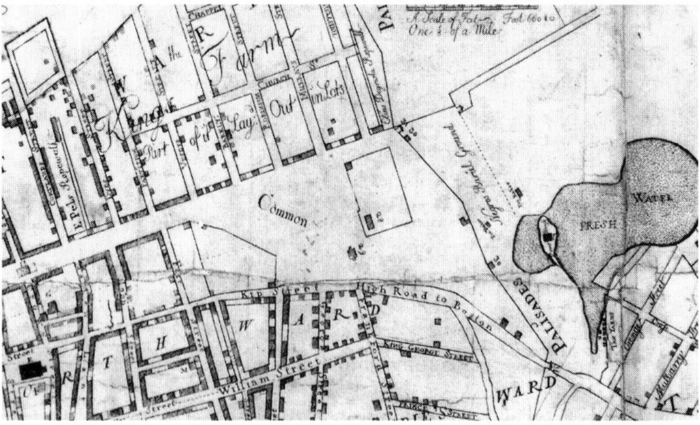

Fig. 2.19. A detail of Maerschalck's "A Plan of the City of New York from an Actual Survey," 1755, showing the location of the "Negros Burial Ground" just to the north of the Common, between the palisades and the Fresh Water Pond, or Collect

slaved people of African descent comes from documents told from the perspective of the city's dominant white community. Thus the discovery of the African Burial Ground has been extremely important in attesting to the presence of enslaved Africans in the city in a vivid, poignant manner. Several women were buried with infants in their arms, for example, suggesting that both had died in childbirth (fig. 2.20).

Although we will probably never know the names of any of the people buried here, scientists like Blakey can build biographies about them. "Burial 101," for example, like most of the people interred in the cemetery, was buried in a coffin. But his coffin was unusual in that it was decorated with a design formed by brass tacks. Excavators initially thought the design represented a heart, but it might also be a Sankofa symbol (fig. 2.21). This symbol, which is derived from the image of a bird and means "turn to the past in order to build the future," is used by the Akan people of Ghana and the Ivory Coast. The remains of Burial 101 show no physical evidence of childhood stress, suggesting that he had a relatively easy childhood, perhaps in Africa. His front teeth were filed into an hourglass shape, a custom practiced in Africa but not among Africans in the Americas. And his vertebrae display fractures that are clearly visible to the naked eye, suggesting, as Blakey put it,

WORKED TO DEATH

The most striking aspect of Blakey's study of the dead in the African Burial Ground is the evidence of the enormous physical hardship suffered by the people interred there. Many appear to have been literally worked to death, as Blakey discovered in his study of the skeletons.

Almost 50 percent of those buried in the Burial Ground were children—a disproportionately high percentage for this time and place. And the infant mortality rate was also very high: of those who died before they were 12 years old, 40 percent were infants. Furthermore, the skeletons of both children and adults show signs of malnutrition and other kinds of physiological stress. Although many of these signs of stress first appear during childhood, a time of growth, their effects are permanent and visible in the teeth and bones of adults. The signs include enamel hypoplasia—horizontal lines visible on the teeth, indicating that growth was interrupted at some point while the tooth was growing, between birth and around 6 years of age for the front teeth. There is also a high incidence of Harris lines—bands of greater bone density in arm and leg bones which are visible on X rays. Harris lines indicate stress, often from malnutrition, during the time of long-bone growth, between birth and approximately 18 years of age. In addition, more than half the population shows signs of infectious disease, including yaws, syphilis, and infectious meningitis. And about half shows evidence of porotic hyperostosis, resulting from severe anemia, which could be from malnutrition, infectious diseases, or sickle-cell disease (most of the enslaved are thought to have come from tropical West Africa, where the population had a high frequency of the sickle-cell trait). And some skeletons exhibit bone deformations indicating rickets and other conditions.

Most revealingly, the teeth and bones of the children uncovered at the Burial Ground are, on the whole, marked by much more developmental stress than those of their elders. Blakey contends that the explanation for this phenomenon could be that many of the adults spent their childhood in freedom in Africa, where life was much less stressful than in colonial New York, where most of the children interred here

> were born enslaved. He estimates that as many as a third of the enslaved in eighteenth-century New York were born in Africa and brought to the city in bondage.
>
> Although we know from historians' research that some of the enslaved worked in highly skilled trades, those who toiled in physical labor worked extremely hard, as their bones tell the Blakey team today. Most adults show signs of enlarged muscle attachments on their arm and leg bones and on their vertebrae. And the bones of many—both men and women— show lesions at the points of muscle attachment. Such lesions form where bone has been literally torn away from bone by excessive muscular strain.

that after his capture and removal to the Americas as an adult "his forced labors were backbreaking in the most literal sense."

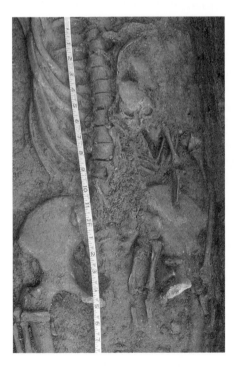

Fig. 2.20. A detail of the burial of a woman, showing her hips and vertebrae. The tiny bones of an infant can be seen on her hip bone.

But his burial in the coffin with what might be a Sankofa symbol suggests that despite his enforced hard labors, he enjoyed respect and prestige in his community.

Another burial found here was of a middle-aged woman. Like many others, she had been wrapped in a shroud and placed in a wooden coffin. But most unusually, a strand of more than a hundred beads encircled her hips. Most of the beads were glass, but two were made of cowrie-like shells that probably came from either the Caribbean or the west African coast. Her front teeth, too, had been filed into traditional African shapes. Although we will probably never know her story, her filed teeth suggest that she was born in Africa, and it is possible

Fig. 2.21. The bird image (*left*) on which the stylized Sankofa image (*right*) is based

that she somehow managed to bring the beaded girdle with her through the infamously cruel Middle Passage. The only other known burial similar to hers from a site in the Americas was that of a man discovered at a plantation in Barbados. He has been identified as an Obeah, or folk doctor. Some think that the woman known today only as Burial 340 may also have been a healer or ritual leader in her community.

Members of today's local African American community have been extremely active in determining the direction of the African Burial Ground project. They fought long and hard, ultimately successfully, both to stop the excavations so that part of the site could be preserved in place and memorialized, and to ensure that the study of the burials be done from an African American perspective and thus supply an African American voice for their ancestors in colonial New York. They are still actively involved in determining how this site will be commemorated and interpreted to the public. The study of the burials is now completed, and the human remains were reburied here in 2003.

Artwork commemorating the African Burial Ground is on display in the lobby of 290 Broadway, the office tower that stands on the site. The African Burial Ground Project maintains an Office of Public Education and Information at 201 Varick Street, Room 1021. For films, programs, and up-to-date information about the African Burial Ground, visit this office, which can be reached at 212-337-1447 or www.africanburialground.com.

Walk back down Duane Street to Centre Street and the Brooklyn Bridge–City Hall subway station, where you can catch the 4, 5, 6, and other subway trains.

The Row, Washington Square North

Tour 3

Greenwich Village At Home in Nineteenth-Century New York

This tour takes you through one of New York's most famous neighborhoods, Greenwich Village (fig. 3.1). You begin in the crooked, picturesque, brownstone-lined streets of the West Village, move east through the once-fashionable Washington Square area, now largely owned by New York University, and on through the tenement-lined streets of the East Village, which are now becoming gentrified. Along the way, you will learn about the Village during the colonial years, when it was rural; find out about the members of the city's wealthy and upper-middle classes who lived near Washington Square when it was one of the city's first residential suburbs; and discover details about the lives of the German and Irish immigrants who lived in the East Village tenements in the late nineteenth century, when the neighborhood was called Kleindeutschland ("Little Germany"). The excavations here have been small in scale, and many were done by university field schools or volunteer teams.

Before the nineteenth century, New York City was located at the southern tip of Manhattan Island. The rest of the island was covered with farms, estates, villages, and—in the seventeenth century—Native American settlements as well. One of the city's many stories is the story of urbanization: how the city swallowed up its hinterland as it grew. Some of the early villages that gave their names to modern city neighborhoods are Harlem, Manhattanville, and Greenwich. This is the story of the village of Greenwich.

During the colonial period, "Greenwich" referred to the area that encompasses today's West Village and included the site of the seventeenth-century Native American settlement Sapokanikan. Today, however, the term "the Village" loosely refers to a large area extending approximately from Houston Street to 14th Street and from the East River to the Hudson. It encompasses three smaller neighborhoods: the West Village, the

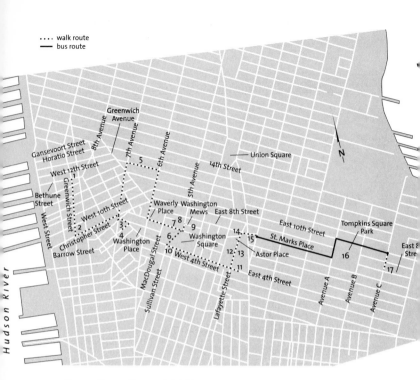

Fig. 3.1. Tour 3: Greenwich Village

Lower Fifth Avenue–Washington Square area (which might be considered today's Greenwich Village), and the East Village (which was formerly considered part of the Lower East Side and is sometimes still thought of that way). This area, two miles north of the colonial city and separated from it by marshland, was called Noortwyck by the Dutch and, later, Greenwich by the English.

The people who lived in this area during the colonial period came from many different walks of life and included some of the city's richest families. The Warrens, Bayards, and DeLanceys all had their estates here. Further to the east, along Bowery Road, were the small farms of the Africans who had been freed from enslavement by the Dutch West India Company, and, later, Bowery Village was situated there. Further east still, in the area known as the East Village today, were the Stuyvesant boweries and other farms, as well as the swampland that lay along the East River.

The transformation that swept New York in the decades after the Revolutionary War had a profound effect on the Village. The city's economy grew astronomically as New York became the primary port of the nation, and the strong economy, in turn, attracted a deluge of migrants and immigrants. There was also a change in the settlement pattern of the city: people who had formerly lived and worked in the same building, and provided room and board there for their workers as well, moved their homes away from their workplaces. This transition resulted in a new demand for real estate, and land values soared. Furthermore, between the 1790s and early 1820s, a number of yellow-fever epidemics swept through the city; the most severe one, in 1798, resulted in the death of 3 percent of the population. As the nineteenth century progressed, the city's downtown business district came to be associated with the large, impersonal economy, the poor, and disease, and therefore was seen by the wealthy and the newly emerging middle class as inappropriate for fostering home life.

The cause of yellow fever was unknown at that time. Some thought that it was contagious, while others thought it was caused by miasmas or vapors emanating from decaying organic matter in the landfill along the East River. It was only much later that people learned that mosquitoes spread the disease. But doctors learned that one effective way to combat an epidemic was evacuation. So healthy New Yorkers were evacuated from those parts of the city where the epidemic raged. At first, the wealthier classes moved to the Village in the summer, as a place of retreat for their families during the epidemic season. They even moved their businesses there temporarily as well. But then came the epidemic of 1822. Whereas the earlier epidemics had begun over by the East River, in areas where the victims were mostly poor, this epidemic began on the West Side, where the city's wealthier families lived. Many of them resolved to move their homes away from the lower city permanently. This decision resulted in the creation of New York City's first suburbs, including Brooklyn Heights and Jersey City (which were both connected to the city by ferries) and Greenwich Village.

In the nineteenth century, today's Washington Square and West Village made up the political ward that was referred to as the "American Ward" because most of its residents were either native born or English-speaking Protestant immigrants. Nonetheless, the area consisted of several different neighborhoods. The winding streets west of Sixth Avenue were home to many middle-class families who made their livings in local shops and trades. Many of those who lived east of Sixth Avenue were much wealthier and included some of the city's more prominent families. This area, made up of some blocks that were positively luxurious and others that were upper middle class, extended east to Second Avenue. The men from these homes commuted downtown on the omnibuses that were introduced in the 1830s to suit their needs. The neighborhood farther to the east had a different character. After the swamps were filled in and the land was developed, much of this part of the East Village became a working-class neighborhood, where the men who worked in the nearby East River shipyards lived with their families. This neighborhood soon became the heart of Kleindeutschland, although many Irish immigrants lived there, too.

Site 1. Greenwich and Bethune Streets: Sapokanikan

Take the A, C, E, or L subway train to 14th Street and Eighth Avenue. Walk south on Eighth Avenue through the meat market, turn right on Bethune Street, and continue to the corner of Greenwich.

In the seventeenth century, before two blocks of landfill stretching from Greenwich to West Streets were added to the Hudson River shore, today's Greenwich Street followed the river's shoreline. Here, between today's Bethune Street and Horatio Street three blocks to the north, was a sheltered cove called Sapokanikan. This was a landing place and probably a trading spot for the Hackensack Indian groups who came to Manhattan to trade. Some of the traders may have come from the interior of New Jersey, crossing the Hudson, which was called Mahikanituk, from today's Hoboken, which was also a trading place at that time. Some think that a trail led from this landing place over to Gansevoort Street and then along the line of today's Greenwich Avenue toward today's Washington Square.

Site 2. Greenwich and West Tenth Streets: Greenwich Mews

Walk south on Greenwich Street five short blocks to West Tenth Street and stop on the southeast corner.

When this housing complex of seven single-family houses was proposed in the mid-1980s, the plans included an underground garage, an amenity requiring a city zoning variance. The zoning variance, in turn, required an environmental review that included an archaeological study, which was conducted by Joan

Fig. 3.2. Hair-dye bottles from the Greenwich Mews site

Geismar. The study revealed that three brick row houses had been built on the block in 1844, and the shafts from the privies of two of these homes were still preserved in the site. The garbage that Geismar found in them reflected some of the ways of life of the middle-class tenants who had lived here in the mid-nineteenth century. The findings included food remains—from beef, fish, shellfish, and fowl—and more-personal items such as Civil War–era photographs—glass plate collodion prints known as ambrotypes, with their images still intact—and bottles that had contained drugs or, for at least one vain soul, hair dye (fig. 3.2).

Site 3. Sheridan Square

Continue south on Greenwich Street to Christopher Street, turn left, and walk east on Christopher to Seventh Avenue. Cross the avenue, turn onto West Fourth Street, and continue to Sheridan Square, the misnomer applied to the triangular garden you see here, formed by the intersection of Barrow and West Fourth Streets and Washington Place.

This is the first site that archaeologists dug in Greenwich Village. Regina Kellerman, director of the Greenwich Village Trust for Historic Preservation, organized the excavation here in 1982 when she realized that the spot where the garden was about to be placed had never been built on before and therefore might hold traces of the village's early history. She knew that Sapokanikan was in the general area and was concerned that gardening activities might destroy the remains of the seventeenth-century Native American landing spot. She contacted archaeologists Anne-Marie Cantwell, Arnold Pickman, and Diana Wall and helped them organize an excavation made up of a team of volunteers consisting of both local Village residents and archaeologists (fig. 3.3). The crew excavated two or three

Fig. 3.3. Volunteers bringing excavation equipment to the Sheridan Square site

days a week throughout the summer and fall. Although they found no traces of Sapokanikan, they did make a rare discovery for lower Manhattan: they uncovered a layer of late eighteenth- and early nineteenth-century topsoil that was underlain by scars left by an early plow—a tangible reminder that before the development of Greenwich Village, the area had been a rural farming community. They also found some refilled holes, all that remained of a line of posts that had once cut across the site. These were aligned with an old property line and could well have been from a fence dividing two eighteenth-century estates owned by neighbors who fought on opposing sides during the Revolutionary War. The loyalist Warren family owned the estate to the north, while the patriot Herring family owned that to the south.

Site 4. 25 Barrow Street

Walk east on West Fourth Street to Barrow Street, turn right, and continue for half a block to 25 Barrow Street.

Located on land that was part of the Herring estate in the eighteenth century, 25 Barrow Street was built in 1826 by mason Jacob Shute as a two-and-a-half-story Federal-style, single-family house. Notice the narrow horse passage along the left side of the house. It leads from the street to the backyard, where, in the mid-nineteenth century, stood a wooden building that was probably a stable. One of the early residents of this house was a cartman who needed a horse and cart for his work. By the mid-nineteenth century the house was home to two and sometimes three separate families.

In 1987, the family that owned the house heard about discoveries that archaeologists were making in the city and alerted Bert Salwen of New York University's anthropology department that they were about to enlarge their kitchen out into the backyard. They were concerned that construction might destroy traces of the Village's past. Salwen (known as the "father of urban archaeology" for his pathbreaking work in the field) knew that their plans might well destroy an underground cistern in their backyard. These brick features, ubiquitous in the early nineteenth century, were used for storing water. Connected by a gutter system to the roof, the cistern was located in the backyard just outside the kitchen so that water could be easily

Fig. 3.4. Dolls found in the cistern at 25 Barrow Street

pumped into the kitchen sink. Salwen, the home-owners, and the construction contractor agreed that if the construction crew found a cistern, they would step aside for a few days and the homeowners would call Salwen, who would organize a dig. The call came, and Salwen, working with students, excavated the feature in four days. They found a layer of coal ash full of artifacts that told them about the lives of the people who lived here when the cistern was filled, around the 1860s.

Two middle-class families rented apartments here at that time. David Sinclair, a locksmith who had a shop around the corner on Bleecker Street, lived here with his wife, Selina, and daughters, Annie and Ellen. And Emeline Hirst, who had moved into the house in 1858 with her husband, Samuel, a baker, lived here with their six children. By 1862 Samuel had died, and the Hirsts had come upon hard times. Emeline and the older children had to support the family; Emeline became a nurse and also took in boarders. Although the strategy of pooling the resources of different family members to support the household usually characterized the way of life of the poor, in Emeline Hirst's case it seems to have been effective in maintaining middle-class status for at least one of her children: her son Edwin became a clerk, the quintessential middle-class profession in late nineteenth-century New York.

Fig. 3.5. An everyday Gothic-style plate from the 25 Barrow Street site

The household goods thrown in the cistern included broken dishes, glassware, and toys like dolls and doll tea sets (fig. 3.4). The dolls may have belonged to Emma Hirst, who was about six years old in 1860, or to Annie and Ellen Sinclair, who were one and three years old, respectively. The dishes showed that like their richer neighbors, Emeline Hirst or Selina Sinclair served family meals on dishes in the Gothic style (fig. 3.5), but they did not use fancy teacups for entertaining their friends, as those neighbors did (see site 5).

Site 5. 153 West 12th Street

Walk back through Sheridan Square to Seventh Avenue. Turn right on the avenue and continue five blocks to 12th Street. Turn right and stop at 153 West 12th Street.

In the 1840s, developers began to build up the northern part of today's West Village with rows of Greek Revival brick and brownstone single-family homes designed for the middle class. Most of these houses continued to be single-family homes until well after the Civil War. This three-story Greek Revival house, which today belongs to the Cooper Union for the Advancement of Science and Art, was built as a single-family home around 1841. In 1855, the 29-year-old Henrietta Raymer and her 37-year-old husband, Henry, moved into the house as tenants; they continued to live there for a decade. Henry Raymer imported groceries, commuting downtown to his business on Front Street. In 1860 the household included the New York–born Raymers, their two young children, George and Maria (aged two and four, respectively), and two servants: Catherine Henn, who had emigrated from Germany, and Anne Hines, who came from Ireland. By 1865 Henry Raymer had died; his widow and young children moved out of the house soon thereafter. We do not know what happened to Henrietta Raymer and her children, but money may have been a problem. The fact that the Raymers did not own their home was unusual for established members of the middle class at that time.

In 1990 Diana Wall led a volunteer crew in excavating the privy shaft behind this house. Like all the nineteenth-century privy pits found in the backyards of Greenwich Village, this one was lined with dry-laid stone, was round in cross-section, and was located just a few feet from the back property line, as far away from the house as possible. This shaft was unusually deep: it extended down more than 12 feet below grade and had to be shored for the excavators' safety.

The excavations on 12th Street revealed that Henrietta Raymer, like the Barrow Street families you visited at site 4, served her family meals on white Gothic-style plates. But unlike the Barrow Street women, she also had gilt-trimmed porcelain teacups in the Italianate style for serving tea to her friends (fig 3.6). These different styles had correlates in the architectural and decorating styles of the day and also in the different roles that were appropriate for middle-class women to play. In the 1840s, the Gothic style became the most popular one for the city's churches, and one of the most important roles for middle-class women was the ecclesiastical one of guarding the morals of the family and society. Middle-class women served meals to their families on Gothic plates in dining rooms decorated with Gothic furniture. At mid-century, the city's architects built row houses in the new, elaborate Italianate style. Advice writers, who were widely read at that time, urged women to use this same elaborate style to furnish their parlors, where they entertained at evening parties designed to help them maintain or shore up their families' position in society.

The tour's next stop is at Sullivan and West Fourth Streets, but you might want to take in a few things along the way. Continue east on 12th Street to Sixth Avenue (officially known as the Avenue of the Americas), turn right, and walk five blocks south to Waverly Place. Turn left on Waverly Place and continue east to Fifth Avenue. After you cross MacDougal Street, **Washington Square (site 6)** is on your right. In 1797 this became the city's potter's field, which it desperately needed to accommodate the victims of the yellow-fever epidemics that were ravaging the city. It is estimated that as many as 22,000 people were buried here in its three decades of use. Even today, workers laying out flower beds and utility lines occasionally find human remains.

Notice also, on your left, the red-brick buildings on Washington Square North. These, built in the 1830s and referred to collectively as **the Row (site 7),** are some of the most distinguished surviving examples of the Greek Revival homes that became the rage in New York in the 1830s. The construction of Washington Square and the Row served to transform the neighborhood into the place that Henry James described in his novel *Washington Square* as embodying "the ideal of quiet and genteel retirement," with an air of "established repose which is not of frequent occurrence in other quarters of the long, shrill city."

Fig. 3.6. An elaborate porcelain teacup and saucer in the Italianate style

Turn left at Fifth Avenue and walk half a block to **2 Fifth Avenue (site 8),** a white brick apartment building with a driveway on the left side of the street. Just inside the lobby of this 1950s building (to the right of the door and visible from the sidewalk) is a fountain consisting of water bubbling in a glass cylinder set on a rectangular marble pedestal. Before the creation of Washington Square, Minetta Brook meandered through the area, surfacing near today's Gramercy Park, running southwest through today's Washington Square, and emptying into the Hudson River near today's Houston Street. The water bubbling in the cylinder is reputed to be from the now-buried brook, which runs under the Fifth Avenue building.

Return to Fifth Avenue and turn right, back toward Washington Square. Here on your left is **Washington Mews (site 9).** Although New Yorkers associate the Washington Square area with the homes of the wealthy families who moved there in the early nineteenth century, they tend to forget that nearby, and often out of sight, were the homes of those who provided services for them. Some were on streets like Washington Mews, today a charming alley lined with picturesque converted coach houses that once belonged to the wealthy families living on Washington Square North and Eighth Street. These coach houses are now prime real estate (many belong to New York University, housing its faculty and administrators), but in the nineteenth century they provided space for carriages and horses and homes for coachmen and other servants.

Site 10. Sullivan and West Fourth Streets

Continue back to Washington Square and walk across the park, heading southwest, to the corner of Sullivan Street and Washington Square South (West Fourth Street). Stop at the southeast corner.

Before 1903, Sullivan Street did not extend as far north as Washington Square; it stopped a block to the south, at Third Street. The area that would later become the continuation of Sullivan Street was covered by houses along both Third and Fourth Streets; these houses were torn down when the street was extended through the block. In 1984, when New York University developed plans to extend the basement of its law school out under Sullivan Street to accommodate its growing library, Bert Salwen and Arnold Pickman led an excavation here, under the street, to see if any archaeological traces sealed under the modern street could reveal details of the ways of life of the people who had lived here in the nineteenth century, before the street was put through.

The buildings that used to stand along Washington Square South were built in the 1820s and consisted of a row of brick Federal houses that were home to many of the wealthier members of the middle class. This side of the square was less expensive than its northern counterpart because it was closer to the poorer neighborhoods developing to the south. Most of the people who lived in the houses on Washington Square South looked out their back windows onto the backs of buildings that became tenements as the century progressed.

The three-story house that was 50 Washington Square South (now on the east side of today's Sullivan Street, right next to New York University's Kevorkian Center) was built in 1826. In 1841 Eliza Robson moved into the house with her husband, Benjamin, a physician who had a practice on East Broadway. They presumably chose the house on Washington Square South to be near their daughter, Mary Sage, and their grandchildren, who lived next door (fig. 3.7). Mary's husband, Francis Sage, was a flour merchant who commuted to his countinghouse downtown. The Robsons continued to live in the house until Benjamin's death almost four decades later.

The archaeologists digging at Sullivan Street discovered the shaft from a privy on the Robsons' property. The contents of this privy were unusual in that they included two separate layers of soil with two separate sets of household goods and other things that had been thrown into the privy at two different times, a decade apart, in the 1840s and the 1850s. These artifacts give us glimpses into the Rob-

Fig. 3.7. Children's mugs from the Robson and Sage homes

sons' home life at two different times. The finds included several sets of dishes. The older sets, those found in the lower layer, were in a style popular in the 1820s and 1830s, and Eliza Robson had probably brought them from her old home when she moved to Washington Square. The more recent dishes, which had become popular in the 1840s, were probably bought after her move uptown. A look at the dishes and glassware from the two layers shows us that tastes changed a lot during these two decades.

When she first moved into the house, Eliza Robson set her table with two different sets of blue-on-white plates decorated with Chinese landscapes (fig. 3.8). This style was very popular at the time, and in fact, her daughter Mary had a set next door that exactly matched one of them. One of the sets was relatively inexpensive. Made of English earthenware, it was decorated with a printed design in the "willow" pattern. The other set, also decorated in the Chinese style, was more expensive—

Fig. 3.8. Plates in the Chinese style from the Robson home: one is made of English earthenware (*left*), and the other of Chinese porcelain

these were porcelain plates imported from China with hand-painted decorations.

The sets of dishes that Eliza Robson bought in the 1840s were very different from the old blue-on-white ones. Like the Raymers on 12th Street and the Barrow Street families, she now preferred solid white plates in the Gothic pattern for family meals, and, like the Raymers, had teacups with gilt trim in the Italianate style for entertaining her friends (see figs. 3.5 and 3.6).

Site 11. 29 East Fourth Street: The Merchant's House Museum

Walk east on Fourth Street for seven short blocks, cross Lafayette Street, and continue on half a block to 29 East Fourth Street, the Merchant's House Museum, one of the city's unheralded treasures. Call 212-777-1089 or visit www. merchantshouse.com for its hours and admission policy. And be sure not to miss the backyard—it didn't always look quite this way.

In some ways the history of the Merchant's House is typical of that of other properties in the Washington Square area. Its small urban lot was once part of a larger farm located outside the city. The farm was subdivided repeatedly as the Village was transformed into a residential suburb. In 1831 Joseph Brewster, a hatter, bought this lot and the one next door. Brewster, like many small-scale developers of his day, built two identical Federal houses on the adjacent parcels. He and his family moved into one of the houses (the one that would later become the Merchant's House) and sold the other. But after living there for only four years, Brewster sold the property to Seabury Tredwell, a successful hardware merchant.

Most early nineteenth-century houses that still stand in New York City were originally built as single-family homes but, like the house on Barrow Street, renovated into multifamily dwellings in the late nineteenth century. (More recently, some of them have been re-renovated back into single-family homes.) But this was not the case here at the Merchant's House. The Tredwell family continued to live here from 1835 until the death of their youngest daughter, Gertrude, in 1933—almost a century later. During the time the family lived there, their fortunes waned, so they did not continually make over their house to keep up with the latest styles. When Gertrude Tredwell, who was known in the neighborhood as an eccentric recluse during the later years of her life, finally died, the house had been relatively untouched for much of a century. After her death, family members led the effort to have the house converted into a museum because they realized that it offered a rare example of upper-middle-class life in the nineteenth-century city.

In 1990, a historic architect asked archaeologist Diana Wall to do an archaeological study of the Merchant's House backyard. She jumped at the chance because she thought that the yard, like the house, might be relatively undisturbed and could provide a rare opportunity to explore the nineteenth-century landscape of an urban garden.

The little that is known about the landscaping of the yards behind middle-class row houses in nineteenth-century New York comes from a handful of architectural plans (fig. 3.9) and real estate advertisements from contemporary newspapers. They show that these gardens were made up of symmetrical planting beds and pathways that provided both pleasant views from house windows and sites for outhouses or privies. Central garden beds were planted with grass, while those along the edges of the backyard contained flowers, shrubs, and climbing vines.

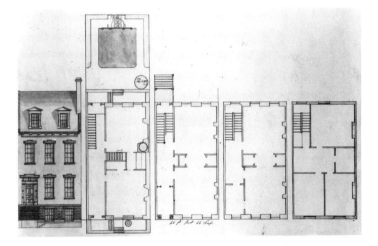

Fig. 3.9. Calvin Pollard's architectural drawing of an early nineteenth-century brownstone, showing its facade (*left*), a plan of each floor, and the backyard plan (above the ground-floor plan)

When the excavations began, the layout of the yard behind the Merchant's House was similar in feeling to the gardens shown in the architectural plans, with two large central planting beds and narrow flower beds along the sides of the garden separated from each other by stone pathways (fig. 3.10). The old outhouse was gone; a raised planting bed in its place at the rear of the garden was a recent addition that the museum had installed in the 1960s.

Working with students from City College, Wall had the main goal of deciphering the layout of the garden during the mid-nineteenth century, when the Brewsters and Tredwells lived here. In many parts of the garden, Wall's team discovered a layer of reddish-brown sand just under the layer of tan sand that was the bedding for the modern stone paths. They analyzed the artifacts in the reddish-brown sand and saw that they all dated to the late eighteenth or early nineteenth century. They realized that this layer of reddish-brown sand was the bedding for the stone pavements of the mid-nineteenth-century garden and that they could use the sand layer as a signature to show them where these nineteenth-century paths had been.

Fig. 3.10. The backyard behind the Merchant's House Museum, 1993

As they plotted the presence and absence of the layer of reddish-brown sand from one area of the excavation to another, the team discovered that the central planting area was much larger in the nineteenth-century garden than it is today (fig. 3.11). And the absence of the sand layer under the path dividing the two central beds showed that there was no path there when the garden was laid out in the 1830s. The original garden may have had one large central planting bed (like the one in the architectural plan shown in fig. 3.9) or the path may have been located elsewhere, further to the north, dividing the original, longer planting area into two planting beds of roughly the same size. But all in all, the modern layout of the yard is quite similar in feeling to that of the nineteenth-century garden.

After you leave the Merchant's House, you might want to take in a few more historic spots in the neighborhood before you catch the bus to the next stop. Walk west, back to Lafayette Street, turn right, and walk north toward Astor Place. This part of Lafayette Street was where many of the city's elite lived during the nineteenth century. About halfway up the block

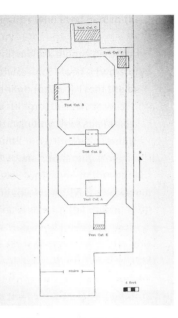

Fig. 3.11. The site map of the backyard behind the Merchant's House. The hatching indicates areas where the archaeologists found the layer of reddish-brown sand.

on the left side of the street is **428–434 Lafayette (site 12),** today a row of dirty-gray buildings with about a dozen columns across its facade. This is the four-building remnant of one of the most elegant rows of houses built in the early nineteenth century. Constructed around 1831 and originally consisting of nine separate buildings, it was called La Grange Terrace (the name came from the estate of the Marquis de Lafayette, who helped the Americans in the Revolutionary War and was still extremely popular decades later). Many of the city's richest families, including the Astors and Vanderbilts, lived here.

Just across the street is today's **Public Theater (site 13),** which was built in the 1850s as the Astor Library, the city's first free library. It later became part of the New York Public Library system.

Continue north to **Astor Place (site 14),** where in May 1849 rioting erupted at the Astor Place Opera House (on the site of today's District 65 Building, at 13 Astor Place on Lafayette). This was the second-deadliest riot in the city's history, the most deadly being the Draft Riots of 1863 (see site 17).

Continue to Eighth Street (which, reflecting its fashionable nineteenth-century history, becomes St. Mark's Place for a few blocks here) and walk a block east to Cooper Square. There, on the south side of St. Mark's, is **Cooper Union (site 15).** This brownstone building was built in 1859 for Peter Cooper, the inventor and manufacturer who established the Cooper Union for the Advancement of Science and Art to provide a free education for workers. Inside is the Great Hall, where many famous people, among them Abraham Lincoln, have spoken over the intervening century and a half.

Walk to the corner of St. Mark's Place (Eighth Street) and catch the M8 bus going east. Along the way, notice **Tompkins Square Park (site 16),** located between Avenues A and B. This park, with its beautiful old trees, was laid out as a public space in 1811 on what had been the estate of Daniel Tompkins, governor of New York State and vice president of the United States. In the early nineteenth century, the park served as a marketplace for farm produce for the people who lived in the area. Throughout much of its history, it has been the site of labor protests, riots, and demonstrations. The most recent was in 1988, when police forcibly removed squatters who were living in the park.

Site 17. 365 East Eighth Street

Get off the bus at Tenth Street and Avenue C and walk two blocks south, to the northeast corner of Eighth Street and Avenue C.

In the nineteenth century, developers built up the area to the east of Tompkins Square in today's East Village with single-family and tenement homes for those who worked in the nearby shipyards located along the East River. After the Civil War, the high costs of both labor and real estate forced most of the yards to move away from New York, and the neighborhood became the site of slaughterhouses, breweries, and coal- and lumberyards, industries that, like the shipyards, required large tracts of land. But even before the decline of the shipbuilding industry there, the neighborhood had begun to change. During the 1840s, large numbers of Irish and German immigrants began to move into New York. By 1855, more than half the population of the 11th Ward, where the shipyards were located, had been born in Germany, and this neighborhood was known as Kleindeutschland. New York was then the city with the third-largest German population in the world.

Samuel Gompers, the founding president of the American Federation of Labor, lived in this neighborhood and worked beside his father as a cigar maker when he was a teenager in the mid-1860s. His memoirs provide a vivid impression of Kleindeutschland: "The house was just opposite a slaughterhouse. All day long we could see the animals being driven into the slaughter pens and could hear the turmoil and the cries of the animals. The neighborhood was filled with the penetrating, sickening odor. The suffering of the animals and the nauseating odor made it physically impossible for me to eat meat for many months after we had moved into another neighborhood."

Today, the building here at the corner of Eighth Street and Avenue C is a large gray four-story police station. It was built in the 1990s on the site of several small mid-nineteenth-century

Fig. 3.12. 365 East Eighth Street in the 1940s

A KLEINDEUTSCHLAND TENEMENT

The four-story tenement at 365 East Eighth Street was built around 1852 in the neighborhood that was quickly becoming Kleindeutschland. In 1864 Joseph Sonnek, a German-born tailor, bought the building from Meyer and Mina Goldsmith, and a few years later he and his family moved into it. In 1870 a total of eight families (including the Sonneks and their three children) lived here. Almost all the adults in these families were immigrants; about half of them came from Germany and the other half from Ireland.

Most of the residents of the Eighth Street tenement worked at skilled occupations: in 1870 all of the German heads of household worked in the tailoring trades and several of their sons worked as cigar makers. The tailors probably worked at home in family shops alongside their wives and children; in the 1850s piece rates were so low that many tailors could not expect to make a living on their own but had to pool their labor with their families'. This way of life was underlined by the German maxim "a tailor is nothing without a wife, and very often a child." Some of the tailors may have worked for their landlord, who by 1880 had built a tailor shop behind the tenement. The Irish tenants and their sons worked as riggers and boilermakers in the shipyards that remained nearby, and their daughters worked at dressmaking and operated sewing machines in factories.

As you can see in the exhibit in the police station, the dishes used in these homes are different from those found at the homes of the wealthier middle-class people on Barrow and West 12th Streets and Washington Square. Although the women of this tenement also liked to set their tables with white plates, few of their plates were in the Gothic pattern. Instead, they seemed to prefer plates that cost about the same but bore such patterns as Bowknot, Huron, Dallas, and Sydenham, which archaeologists have not found at middle-class sites in the Village. It seems that these immigrant women had different tastes in plates from their more established, American-born, middle-class neighbors to the west.

tenements. Before it was built, Joel Grossman led an excavation here, in the backyard behind the tenement at 365 East Eighth Street, about a quarter of the way down the block (fig. 3.12). He and his crew discovered a privy shaft containing thousands of artifacts. Many of them are on view in the eleven windows that line the Avenue C and Eighth Street sides of the police station; the exhibit continues in the building's lobby, which is open to the public. Taken together, they give us a surprisingly intimate look into the households of immigrant families settling into their new country.

To return to major north-south transportation routes, go back to Tenth Street and Avenue C and catch either the M8 bus, which goes west on 9th Street, or the M14, which goes north on Avenue C to 14th Street and then west to Union Square and beyond.

The salt marsh at Inwood Hill Park

Tour 4

Northern Manhattan How the First Archaeologists Uncovered
Indian, Colonial, and Revolutionary War New York

This tour (fig. 4.1) takes you to Inwood in northern Manhattan.
Here you will follow in the century-old footsteps of the pioneering archaeologists who explored the lives of peoples of Native American, European, and African descent, including those
of the British and Hessian soldiers stationed here during the
Revolutionary War. As you travel through a splendid city park,
a quiet middle-class residential neighborhood, and a bustling
semi-industrial area, you will imagine Inwood's rural landscape
at the beginning of the twentieth century, when these archaeologists were digging and the area was being transformed into
the parks and streets you see today.

In the early twentieth century, Manhattan's growing population was spreading up to Inwood, at the island's northern tip.
In the eastern part, as in so many other city neighborhoods,
the subway was the harbinger of change. The elevated 1 train,
which runs along Tenth Avenue, opened around 1906, and the
flatter farmlands there were transformed into streets lined
with apartment buildings designed for immigrant Irish and
Eastern European Jewish families, members of the city's working class. They are now home to new generations of immigrants, including many from Latin America. Somewhat later,
workers began to raze the estates that lay west of Broadway,
in the hilly part of Inwood, and to grade the land and lay out
streets that would soon be lined with apartment buildings
designed for the middle class. But before these changes took
place, most of Inwood was rural. In fact, there was so much
empty space that gypsies used to camp here for weeks at a
time. The only part of Inwood that still looks somewhat as it
did before the arrival of urbanization is Inwood Hill Park,
which the city acquired in 1916.

When construction workers were altering the landscape,

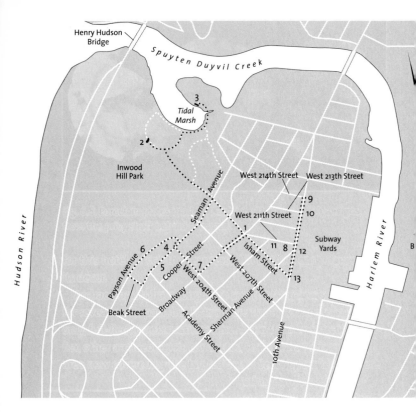

Fig. 4.1. Tour 4: northern Manhattan

several New Yorkers who cared about the city's history became concerned. They saw that development was destroying the archaeological traces of the city's past, with no objections from city officials or even its cultural institutions. Two of them, Reginald Pelham Bolton and William L. Calver, both engineers by profession, decided to take matters into their own hands and salvage what they could of the city's history. They saw themselves as explorers, for whom saving the past was a civic duty. Sometimes joined by like-minded citizens or by family members, they devoted their weekends to their expeditions. Unlike most archaeologists today, they were very formal in their ways: they always addressed each other as Mr. Calver and Mr. Bolton in the frequent letters they exchanged, and, weather permitting, they excavated in white shirt, coat, and tie. At first they focused on Native American sites, but as they discovered more and more colonial and Revolutionary War sites, they began excavating those as well.

Around the time that Calver and Bolton were at work, two archaeologists from the Museum of the American Indian, Alanson Skinner and Amos Oneroad, were also digging Native American sites in upper Manhattan, including a major one in Inwood Hill Park. Skinner had grown up in Staten Island and had spent much of his youth digging there before he went to Columbia University. Oneroad, a member of the Menomini people, was one of the first Native American archaeologists in the country.

Much of what we know about the archaeological past in this part of the city comes from the pioneering efforts of these four men. And although their techniques were not on a par with those used by archaeologists today, their work provides the major archaeological evidence that we have for the events that took place in northern Manhattan before it became part of the urban landscape.

Site 1. Broadway and Isham Street

Take the A subway train to Inwood–207th Street and Broadway. When you exit the station, walk one block north on Broadway to Isham Street.

This busy intersection was part of a substantial Indian settlement in Woodland times (between 2,700 and 400 years before present, or B.P.). Skinner and Oneroad found its traces when they were digging here in March 1919. They discovered a number of ancient trash pits filled with refuse from food—discarded deer, muskrat, and fish bones, oyster and clam shells, lobster claws, and fragments of broken pottery.

Site 2. Inwood Hill Park's Shorakapok Rock

Turn left on Isham Street and walk two blocks west to Seaman Avenue and the entrance to Inwood Hill Park. The park is one of the city's marvels, with rugged schist outcrops that rise up to 200 feet and the last natural forest and tidal marsh left in Manhattan. Legend has it that this area was known as Shorakapok to the Native Americans who lived here. Take the path to Shorakapok Rock (see fig. 4.1).

As the plaque here indicates, this rock marks the spot where a great tulip tree once stood. Some people think it also marks the spot where Peter Minuit, the director general of the Dutch West India Company, allegedly bought the island of Manhattan from the resident Munsee Indians for baubles worth $24.

The area near where you are standing was home to Native Americans for thousands of years. As you look around, you can see that this is an ideal spot for a settlement. It is a sheltered valley, with a freshwater spring nearby and easy access, via the Spuyten Duyvil Creek (now considerably widened), to both the Hudson and Harlem Rivers and points beyond. When Indians lived here, there were abundant resources nearby, especially at those times of the year when shad, sturgeon, striped bass, and other fish were running. Oysters and other shellfish would have been available year round, deer and smaller game could be hunted in the adjacent wooded areas, and a variety of vegetable foods, including highly nutritious nuts, were easily accessible.

We know that the Native Americans exploited the resources of this rich tidewater environment because when Skinner and Oneroad were digging here in the fall of 1918 they found extensive shell middens stretching down to the shore. They also discovered some ancient hearth pits where food was cooked, as well as other pits, many measuring up to four feet in diameter, where food was stored or refuse tidily thrown away. They found

THE SELLING OF MANHATTAN

A close look at the popular American myth surrounding the sale of Manhattan in 1626 shows that it, like so many myths, is not true. The only evidence for this sale is a letter to the Netherlands that somewhat off-handedly comments that the Dutch "bought the island of Manhates from the Wild Men for the value of sixty guilders." We don't know what was given to the Munsees for the "value of sixty guilders" (or who gave it), but it is highly likely that the Munsees did not believe that by accepting these objects they were selling their land in the European sense, that is, permanently giving up the right to live on it. Instead, they probably believed that they were allowing visitors to use it temporarily. For the Munsees, land was seen as held in trust for the Creator, Kishelemulong, and as such could never be sold or even owned.

In upper Manhattan, Native American peoples continued to hunt in their traditional hunting grounds and plant maize in their traditional fields near the Spuyten Duyvil Creek, and even perhaps near Isham and 207th Streets, late into the seventeenth century. There are also accounts of Indians still living here in later years, including one that places some in Inwood as recently as 1817.

fragments of pottery, broken cups and dishes carved from turtle shell, discarded spear and arrow points, fishing plummets, a bone harpoon point, and a variety of other tools (fig. 4.2).

We don't know what kind of houses these early residents of Inwood built for themselves in this sheltered spot. Some might have lived in round single-family wigwams; others may have inhabited multifamily longhouses; and still others may have taken shelter among the numerous large overhanging rocks along the southern slope of the hills, as some modern New Yorkers do today. The excavation techniques available to Skinner and Oneroad in 1918 didn't allow them to identify the Indians' dwellings. And unfortunately, there is much more we will never know about this important site because, as Skinner

Fig. 4.2. Some of the artifacts found at Inwood: (*top left*) pipes, (*top right*) a face pendant, and (*bottom*) a pottery sherd

bemoaned when he was digging here, even then, in the first quarter of the twentieth century, large portions of the site, including the rock shelters, had already been destroyed by over thirty years of digging and looting.

Nevertheless, Skinner and Oneroad made important discoveries. They found evidence not only of daily domestic routines but also of ancient ceremonies that took place in this sheltered valley. Hints of these rituals came from a number of broken smoking pipes (see fig. 4.2). The people here may have been smoking native tobacco, *Nicotiana rustica* (which is stronger than the kinds common today) or other plants, including hemp, sumac, and fleabane flowers. These plants and the act of smoking itself were part of widespread rituals that even today, centuries later, are still important in many Native American ceremonies.

Other finds give us a more intimate view of these early residents. Skinner and Oneroad discovered several ornaments or amulets, including pendants made of bone and stone, which were strung and worn around the neck. Among the most unusual was one that depicted a human face (see fig. 4.2).

You might want to follow some of the paths that go around

the hill. The one marked Spuyten Duyvil Road has a splendid view of the tidal marsh and the junction of Spuyten Duyvil Creek and the Hudson River, just beyond the Henry Hudson Bridge.

Site 3. Inwood Hill Nature Center

Leaving Shorakapok Rock, walk around the tidal marsh (where you might see nesting swans, as well as egrets and ducks) to the Inwood Hill Nature Center. The center has small but interesting displays on the importance of tidal marshes, local geology, and the people who once lived here. Call 212-304-2365 for hours and information about special programs.

Site 4. Seaman Avenue at 204th Street

Exit the park at the Isham Street entrance, turn right on Seaman Avenue, and walk south. Near the park's entrance, Bolton found a number of Indian artifacts and refuse pits and suggested that this area might have been a Native American planting field. Indian artifacts have been found all along Seaman Avenue, and hearths from ancient fires have been found on the ridges of Inwood Hill.

Continue to the corner of 204th Street. Refer to Bolton's map (fig. 4.3) to locate some of the archaeological discoveries that he and Calver made here a century ago, when this was farmland. Here, at the corner where you are standing, was a freshwater spring. Down at the end of the block, near Academy Street, was a large apple and pear orchard, and a manse stood at the corner. But there were also workmen swarming everywhere, grading for streets, putting in sewers, and transforming the land into the quiet residential area it is now. Along this block, the workers turned up the remains of both a substantial Late Woodland settlement (ca. 1,000–400 B.P.) and a British and Hessian Revolutionary War camp, which extended over to Payson Avenue to the west. Bolton and Calver began to salvage what they could of the remnants of these two important periods in the neighborhood's history (fig. 4.4).

Construction workers destroyed much of the Native American settlement that once stood here along Seaman Avenue. And as at Inwood Hill Park, the way the archaeologists dug the site leaves us no evidence of precisely where the Native Ameri-

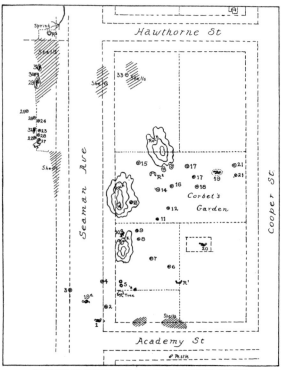

LOCATION OF BURIALS, PITS AND SHELL BEDS NEAR INWOOD

1. Human remains. 2. Shell pit, deer antler. 3. Shell pit. 4. Shell pit, pottery. 5. Shell pits 6. Shell pit, sturgeon below. 7. Shell pit, sturgeon scales. 8, 9. Shell pits. 10. Human remains. 11. Fire pit. 12. Shell pit. 13. Dog burial, puppy. 14. Shell pit. 15. Part of a jar. 16. Shell pit, fish and meat bones. 17. Shell pits. 18. Two dogs in shell pit. 19. Human skeleton, 1907. 19a. Female skeleton, 1908. 20. Human remains when house was built. 21. Small fire pits, Revolutionary. 22. Large shell pit. 23. Large shell pit. 24. Shell pit. 25. Dog burial. 26, 27, 28. Shell pits. 29. Two human skeletons, male and female. 30. Revolutionary fireplace "Royal Marines" and "17th." 31. Skeleton female, and infant. 32. Skeleton (Chenoweth, 1908). 33. Revolutionary fireplace. 71st, officers' buttons. D. Dyckman dwelling. R¹, R². Revolutionary fireplaces. R³. Revolutionary well.

Fig. 4.3. Bolton's map of the discoveries at the Seaman Avenue site. Hawthorne Street is now West 204th Street.

can houses stood or how they were fashioned. But we can certainly make some inferences. As you see from Bolton's map, the archaeologists found a number of trash and storage pits as well as hearths, which the Native Americans had probably placed near their houses. The household refuse they threw out in the trash pits tells us that they were eating clams and oysters, various kinds of fish, venison, and such vegetable foods as corn and acorns.

The most spectacular finds the archaeologists made on

Fig. 4.4. An early twentieth-century photograph showing a shell pit at the Seaman Avenue site

this block open up a window into important and little-known parts of the social and spiritual lives of the peoples who lived here so many centuries ago. Near where you are standing, on the west side of Seaman near 204th Street where large prewar apartment buildings now stand, Bolton and Calver salvaged and recorded a number of human burials as they were being destroyed. Contemporary accounts describe workmen shoveling through and discarding many of these Indian burials, the first to be discovered in Manhattan.

The burial shown on Bolton's map as number 29 (near top left) was a double burial (see fig. 4.3). Bolton and Calver first discovered an adult male, who was in his mid-thirties when he died. Upon his right arm, someone had placed a compact bundle of human bones, apparently charred, of an adult female also in her mid-thirties. They were puzzled by their discovery and speculated about its meaning. Today, we know that this practice—known as a secondary, bundle, or bone burial—is common throughout the world. In secondary burials, human skeletal remains are removed from their original or primary grave, gathered together in a bundle, and reburied elsewhere. Europeans living in the area during the seventeenth century wrote that among some Native American peoples, if someone died and

was buried far from home, it was customary to disinter the
bones later and bring them back home and rebury them there.
So it is possible that this woman died far away from what is
now Seaman Avenue and was buried in some distant place, and
that later her bones were gathered up to be reburied with this
man, perhaps her husband, on the occasion of his funeral in
their home settlement, near where she had once lived.

Right near this burial, Bolton and Calver salvaged another
grave that hints at an equally poignant, centuries-old drama
(see number 31 on fig. 4.3). This was also a double burial, in this
case that of an adult woman and an infant. In excavating this
burial, the archaeologists noticed a stone arrowhead that appeared to have been dislodged from an area near the woman's
rib cage—it may well have been the cause of her death, but we
do not have enough information to know for sure. We also have
no way of knowing the cause of the infant's death. Like all the
other burials at this settlement, this one was carefully covered
with a layer of shell—probably, as Bolton thought, to protect it
from predators.

Site 5. Seaman Avenue: Dog Burials and the Soldiers' Summer Camp

Continue walking down Seaman Avenue, stopping halfway
down the block, at the approximate location of Corbet's Garden

Fig. 4.5. A dog burial at Seaman Avenue

on Bolton's map (see fig. 4.3). As you walk down the avenue, note that there were a number of shell pits on your left, indicating that a Late Woodland house may have once stood there.

Along this stretch of Seaman Avenue, Bolton and Calver made a series of startling discoveries of funerary ceremonies. They found eleven burials of dogs (fig. 4.5). Each dog was buried in the same way that humans were at that time: placed in a burial pit and then covered with shell. Several of these were found in the area marked Corbet's Garden. Here Bolton also

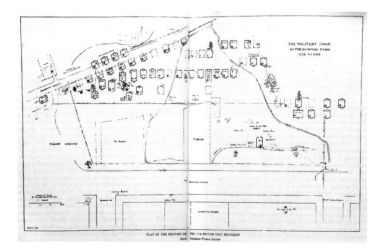

Fig. 4.6. Bolton's map of the Revolutionary War camp at Payson Avenue

"I AM ONLY A DOG"

Clues to why the dogs were buried here come from the lives of modern-day Delaware Indians, the descendants of the Late Woodland and Munsee peoples who lived here so many centuries ago. A dog was traditionally given to a Delaware child not only as a pet, but more important, as that child's vicar or surrogate. The parents hoped that the animal would attract any sickness and spare the child from illness. These guardian dogs were thought to believe, "I am only a dog. The child is more precious." If the guardian dog died, it was often said to have died in the child's place and was buried with loving care, as humans were. Dogs were believed to help adults in similar ways. It may be that the dogs discovered here on the eastern edge of Inwood Hill and at sites in the other boroughs had once served as vicars for the humans whose lives they had shared and whose diseases they had borne. Apparently, not all dogs served as surrogates, however. Many were not carefully buried but simply thrown on the garbage heap.

THE REVOLUTIONARY WAR

In August 1776 the British fleet, armed with 1,200 cannon and carrying 32,000 troops and 13,000 seamen, massed in the Narrows off the coast of Staten Island. Over the course of the next two months, the British conquered the city, which they continued to control until the very end of the war, in 1783. New York was the only American city to be occupied by the British for almost the entire duration of the Revolutionary War.

Strategically, northern Manhattan was extremely important for both sides, because it guarded the city from attacks from the north. At the beginning of the war, the Americans prepared for British attack by building extensive fortifications there as well as throughout the New York area. After taking the city and establishing it as the base of their operations in the warring colonies, the British in turn expanded these fortifications and stationed thousands of British and Hessian troops there.

came upon the grave of two young dogs buried together in a position that he described as "nose to tail."

Here at Corbet's Garden and along Seaman Avenue, Calver and Bolton not only found evidence of the Native American past but also discovered traces of a British and Hessian military camp from the Revolutionary War (fig. 4.6; see also fig. 4.3). Starting in 1912, the archaeologists dug at the site for years. They discovered that the camp extended over to Payson Avenue to the west and Cooper Street to the east.

The soldiers who camped here were probably attracted by the same features that had appealed to the Native Americans before them. The flatter land just to the east of Inwood Hill, on either side of Seaman Avenue and extending down to Cooper Street, was ideal for camping in the summer, when the soldiers probably lived in tents. There Bolton and Calver discovered some fire pits and fireplaces that were left from these summer quarters.

Site 6. Payson Avenue: The Soldiers' Winter Camp

Continue walking down Seaman Avenue past Academy Street, turn right on Beak Street, and right again on Payson Avenue. It was here, along Payson Avenue and in the apple and pear orchard to its east, that Bolton and Calver made some of their richest discoveries of the Revolutionary War years: the huts that were the soldiers' winter quarters (fig. 4.7; see also fig. 4.6).

Fig. 4.7. The military camp as imagined by John Ward Dunsmore in 1915

As you look at the lower slope of the hill, you can see why it was so enticing in the winter. The southeastern-facing slope not only caught the warmth of the sun but also gave protection against prevailing westerly winds. And the soil was well drained, so that the soldiers' huts, which were semi-subterranean and built into the hillside, were not damp. The floors were of hard-packed dirt, although there were some less-compacted sandy areas over near the walls, perhaps where beds had been. The archaeologists often found decayed straw, which may have served as bedding, in that area. The huts had pitched roofs, probably made of lumber, as were the gable ends. Over the years, the archaeologists excavated more than 50 of the 60 huts they found (fig. 4.8). In 1915 Calver and Bolton reconstructed one of these huts in the backyard of the Dyckman Farmhouse, where it can be seen today (see site 7).

The scores of artifacts that Bolton, Calver, and their helpers found illuminate the lives of the soldiers in these camps during these critical years in the nation's history. On the floor of one hut, for example, Bolton and Calver found the remnants of what had probably been a vest along with seven small silver buttons inscribed 17, for the 17th Regiment. Right nearby was a brass pin, a pair of tailor's scissors, and a thimble. Bolton sur-

Fig. 4.8. Bolton (*standing*) and Calver examining a fireplace in one of the huts

mised that the hut's last occupant was a regimental tailor who
was doing some mending when he had to abandon his home.
At another hut, the excavators discovered a large pile of broken
liquor bottles on the floor along with an iron funnel. Together,
these artifacts suggested that this hut may have served as a
canteen where soldiers obtained liquor.

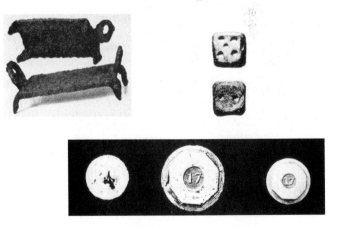

Fig. 4.9. Some of the artifacts found at the Revolutionary War camp:
(*top left*) ice creepers, (*top right*) dice, and (*bottom*) buttons

Other artifacts evoke the hardships of war and the daily life of the times. Ice creepers, which were attached to shoes to give traction for moving about on the ice, were found in most of the huts (fig. 4.9). They remind us of the incredibly hard winter of 1779–80, when the Hudson River froze over and the East River filled with floating ice. Other discoveries were related to arms, like the mold for making lead musket balls and the musket balls themselves, with hand-wrought nails embedded in them for ravaging enemy flesh. And there were traces of the soldiers' domestic lives: pieces of pottery from the dishes they used, shells and bones from their food, and the ubiquitous fragments of liquor bottles. The archaeologists also discovered evidence of the tedium of life in the huts: they found the musket balls that the soldiers had turned into dice to use in games of chance. Dice like these have been found at many military sites throughout the region (see fig. 4.9).

Site 7. Broadway and 204th Street: The Dyckman Farmhouse Museum

Follow Payson Avenue north (see fig. 4.6 for the location of the huts), until it loops back to Seaman Avenue. Turn right, then take a sharp left onto 204th Street, and go two blocks to Broadway. The Dyckman Farmhouse Museum is at the northeast corner of 204th Street and Broadway. Call 212-304-9422 or visit www.dyckman.org for the museum's hours and admission policy. Note the house's elevation in relation to modern-day Broadway—a vivid reminder of how the grading that preceded development in the early twentieth century dramatically altered the landscape here and, in the process, destroyed a myriad of archaeological sites.

This house, the only eighteenth-century farmhouse still standing in Manhattan, was built by William Dyckman after the Revolutionary War. The Dyckmans were an important landowning family in northern Manhattan during the colonial period. Jan Dyckman emigrated from Westphalia in 1662 along with his friend Jan Nagel. The land that they held together extended north from 211th Street to Spuyten Duyvil Creek. In 1690, after Jan Dyckman and Rebecca Nagel had each become widowed, they married each other and thus kept the property intact. Dyckman continued to acquire land so that at his death in 1715, the joint estate totaled three hundred acres. After his wife's death in 1719, all this land was divided among the Dyckman and Nagel children. Two step-brothers, Jacobus Dyckman and Jan Nagel, bought out many of their siblings and together came to own more than two hundred acres, which in 1744 they divided, using 211th Street as the boundary between their properties. Dyckman took the southerly parcel and Nagel the northerly.

William Dyckman and his family, like many patriots, left British-occupied Manhattan for the duration of the war. When they returned, they discovered that the British had destroyed their house, which had been located near 208th Street and Ninth Avenue (see site 13), along with their barns and orchards. The Dyckmans rebuilt their house here, on the King's Bridge Road (now Broadway), a major artery to the mainland. Jacobus Dyckman, William's son, inherited the farm in 1787 and continued to live here with his family, adding considerably to the property. The family sold the house in the 1870s, but two descendants bought it back when developers threatened to raze it; they donated it to the City of New York in 1916.

In addition to rooms furnished in early nineteenth-century style, the farmhouse has a Relic Room, with a display of many of the artifacts that Bolton and Calver found in the area as well as photographs of their excavations. (Some artifacts are also on display in the Luce Center at the New-York Historical Society.)

Behind the house, a remnant of the original Dyckman property has been turned into a pleasant garden where, in 1915, Bolton and Calver reconstructed one of the military huts that they had excavated on Payson Avenue. If you peer through the windows of the hut you can see a fireplace, bed, table, and bench, all thought to be typical of the quarters of the British and Hessian soldiers who camped here during the Revolution.

Site 8. Tenth Avenue at 211th Street

Exit the museum, go north on Broadway to Isham Street, take a right, and walk down the slope to Tenth Avenue. Turn left and continue in the shadow of the elevated tracks of the 1 train to 211th Street. Today this section of the west side of Tenth Avenue is lined with used car lots, automotive stores, and other small businesses, while on the east side are the city's massive Subway Yards. Although it may be hard to imagine today, right here is

Fig. 4.10. Net sinkers found in upper Manhattan

where Bolton and Calver made some of the first discoveries in Manhattan of the lives of Indians, early colonists, enslaved Africans, and Revolutionary War soldiers.

In 1904, when this was still a rural area and these streets were being laid out, workmen began to raze a knoll just to the west of Tenth Avenue, between 210th and 211th Streets, so that the soil could be used to level nearby streets. When the knoll was cut down to the level of the surrounding fields, Bolton and Calver found about a dozen shell pits that appeared to be arranged in a semicircle around it. Each pit was about three feet across and as many feet deep, and contained four or five bushels of oyster shell. At the base of one of these pits was a complete skeleton of a dog accompanied by a few pieces of broken pottery. Two of the other pits each held the complete skeleton of a snake, one of which was about two and a half feet long, and a fourth pit contained the remains of a turtle. Bolton and Calver were convinced that this was an ancient ceremonial site, a sacred space where great tribal rituals had once been held.

One of the reasons for their conclusion was that some years earlier, in 1895, Calver had made similar finds nearby. He had discovered two dog burials further to the east, on a ridge not far from the Harlem River, on the site of today's Subway Yards. One of the burials was near 209th Street, and the other, near 210th Street. Like the other burials in upper Manhattan at this time, these dogs had been placed in pits that were then capped with oyster shells.

Separated and distinct from these two dog burials, and closer to the Harlem River shore, Calver found a large Native American shell-refuse deposit containing various discarded tools, including fishing net sinkers (fig. 4.10). There was obviously a substantial Native American settlement here along the shoreline at one time, but unfortunately, we know little about it or its relationship to the ceremonial pits.

Site 9. Tenth Avenue at 214th Street

Walk up Tenth Avenue to 214th Street and cross to the east side of the avenue.

Fig. 4.11. Calver examining the pot he discovered on 214th Street near Tenth Avenue

You are now near the spot where Calver discovered one of the best-preserved Indian pots ever found in Manhattan (figs. 4.11 and 4.12). He found this extraordinary pot on the south side of 214th Street, about 150 yards east of where you are now on Tenth Avenue. While out on one of his relic-hunting walks in November 1906, he noticed that a recent rain had exposed something in a hillock that had just been graded. He thought at first that it was a boulder, but that seemed odd since it was lying in a bed of otherwise clear fine sand. He tapped the mysterious object with his knuckles and realized that he had discovered a beautifully made Late Woodland jar, about 13½ inches in diameter and the same in height, fired black, and lying on its side.

There was an additional surprise in store. After Calver had carefully removed the pot, he noticed that the side it had been lying on had a hole punched through it near the base. The pot appeared to have been deliberately buried in the hillock, perhaps for ceremonial reasons. There were also some

Fig. 4.12. The curious pot found at 214th Street

traces of charcoal nearby. Today archaeologists would say that the pot had been "killed"—which is what they call artifacts that were intentionally broken into pieces or punched with holes and then buried in graves or other ceremonial precincts. For many peoples in various parts of the world, these deliberately broken objects are, in effect, dead; they have no use to the living. This ritual "killing" can be done to release the spirit of the artifact, prevent its improper use, or claim it for the dead or for the spiritual world. But any evidence that might help us understand more about this pot that was so beautifully crafted, deliberately defaced, and then carefully buried, has long since been destroyed by modern development.

Site 10. 213th Street and Tenth Avenue

Walk back one block on Tenth Avenue to 213th Street by the Subway Yards.

In 1906, Bolton and Calver discovered the remains of a house along the Harlem River, near 213th Street, to the east of the Subway Yards there now. All that was left was a 13-by-16-foot cellar that could be entered by descending a short flight of stone steps that led down about four feet below modern grade. Along one wall was a brick fireplace. The walls were stone and the floor paved with bricks, although many of them had been removed. Bolton and Calver thought that they had found the remains of the house that Tobias Teunissen, the first European known to have lived in this area, had built in 1640 at a time when Native Americans were still living and working here.

In 1736, Jan Nagel, who then owned the property, built another house, now known as the Century House, nearby. During the Revolutionary War, when his three unmarried sons were living in the house, it served as British officers' quarters, which perhaps explains why it was not destroyed in the war. When the house burned down in 1903, an antiquarian took the lintel, inscribed with the words "J. N., May 23, 1736"; it is now in the Dyckman Farmhouse Museum (see site 7).

At the beginning of the twentieth century, when workers were grading the area east of these Nagel homes for the opening of 212th Street, they destroyed some graves that lay in the path of the new street. These graves were part of a burial

THE TEUNISSEN FARMHOUSE

Tobias Teunissen, a woolwasher by trade, had emigrated from the Netherlands in 1636 and four years later built his house along the Harlem River. In 1655 the so-called Peach War began after a Dutch settler shot and killed a Native American woman for taking a ripe peach from his orchard. A series of deadly attacks and counterattacks followed, and in one of them some Indians attacked Teunissen's farm, killed him, and took his widow and only surviving child, Teunis, captive. They were released several weeks later but did not return to the farm. In 1677 the British colonial government re-granted Teunissen's land to two local landowners, Jan Dyckman and Jan Nagel. After their deaths, their children divided the property. Nagel's son, also named Jan, took the part that included the old Teunissen farmhouse and apparently incorporated part of it into the home he built here. Revolutionary War soldiers seem to have used the house later in the eighteenth century, because in the basement Bolton and Calver found hoops from barrels that may have held their flour, liquor, or gunpowder, as well as two bayonets and the hammers of flintlock muskets. They also discovered two 16-pound bar shot in the fireplace. Each bar shot consisted of two iron balls connected by an iron rod. These were probably used as andirons, a practice common at the time.

ground where the Nagels, Dyckmans, and other Inwood families buried their dead from colonial times through the nineteenth century. The cemetery was located on high ground and extended from 213th Street down to approximately the middle of 212th Street, in the area now incorporated into the Subway Yards.

Local families used the western part of the cemetery, closer to Tenth Avenue. Legend had it that the graves in the eastern, older part of the cemetery, which had unmarked rough stones indicating the head and feet of each grave, were the final resting places of Hessian soldiers. Bolton and his helpers opened one of these graves and found a skeleton, which they identified as that of a man, buried about five feet deep in a cedar coffin, which had been put together with hand-forged nails. The nails convinced them that the burial was from the colonial period, but they could not confirm that the man had been a soldier. Later on, in the 1920s, workers excavating for the Subway Yards destroyed the cemetery, which was by then neglected, but not before 417 bodies were disinterred. The Board of Transportation arranged for their reburial in Woodlawn Cemetery in the Bronx. But before their reburial, Harry Shapiro, a physical anthropologist at the American Museum of Natural History, was able to study some of the skeletons in 1926. His analysis showed, among other things, that the average height of the men he studied was five feet six inches, slightly taller than the average height of a sample of men who lived in London in the seventeenth century, who measured in at a mean of five feet five inches, and slightly shorter than European American Civil War recruits, who averaged five feet eight inches.

Site 11. 211th Street and Tenth Avenue

Continue walking back down Tenth Avenue to 211th Street. There on the right, just to the west, was the knoll around which Bolton and Calver found the Native American ceremonial site that included the burial pits with a dog, two snakes, and a turtle (site 8). But earlier, the archaeologists had made another remarkable discovery on the top of this very same knoll.

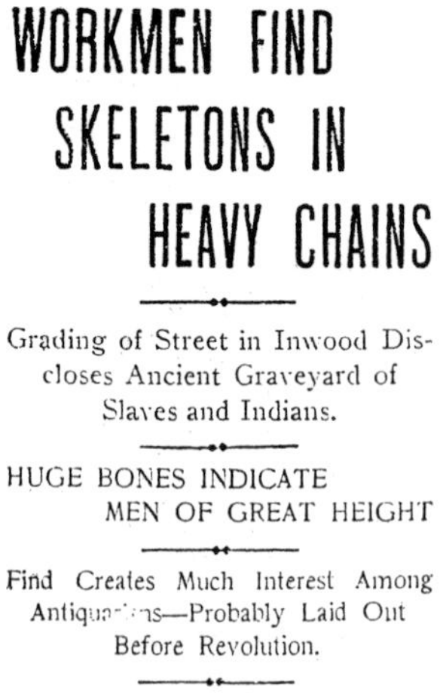

James Finch, another enthusiastic avocational archaeologist, who coincidentally was also an engineer, recorded the events surrounding the exploration of what proved to be an African burial ground found in a grove of trees on the knoll that then rose 12 feet above Tenth Avenue. One Saturday in March 1903, sensa-

WORKMEN FIND SKELETONS IN HEAVY CHAINS

Grading of Street in Inwood Discloses Ancient Graveyard of Slaves and Indians.

HUGE BONES INDICATE
MEN OF GREAT HEIGHT

Find Creates Much Interest Among Antiquans—Probably Laid Out Before Revolution.

Fig. 4.13. Headlines from the *Evening Telegram*, March 14, 1903, announcing the discovery of the cemetery

tional reports appeared in local newspapers describing the discovery of a burial ground that workmen had found on top of the hill (fig. 4.13). They said that some of the dead had been buried upright, with balls and chains hanging from their limbs. They also mentioned that a man who had grown up in the neighborhood reported that as a child he had heard that the slaves of the Dyckmans and other local families had buried their dead in this cemetery. The next day Finch, together with Calver, investigated the cemetery. They quickly discovered that the story of the upright burials was false; the only iron ball that had been found was a cannonball, which had turned up a hundred yards away from the cemetery. But they agreed that the burial ground was in fact a cemetery for the enslaved.

Before emancipation in 1827, slave labor played an important role in the economy of most of the rural areas around New York City, particularly on the farms where Dutch-Americans lived. The Dutch-American homes of Inwood were no exception. In 1790, about 40 percent of the households in the rural parts of Manhattan Island, to the north of the city, included slaves.

The archaeologists determined that the burial ground included 36 graves arranged in rows, each marked by an uncut stone at its head, which was oriented to the west. They found pieces of decayed wood and rusty nails, all that remained of the coffins, and brass pins, suggesting that the dead had been buried in shrouds. Calver reportedly bought a skull from a workman that showed "a very peculiar and abnormal development of the teeth." There was also a poignant report of a child who had been buried with a bead necklace.

The following Saturday, Finch brought Ales Hrdlicka, a renowned physical anthropologist at the American Museum of Natural History, to examine the cemetery. He confirmed that the four skulls that he saw were in fact "negro." Although a local police captain had directed that the bones be "decently re-buried," no one, apparently, saw to it. Instead, some of the skulls were treated with what to our eyes today would be shocking callousness. They ended up in the hands of collectors, workers, and people who lived in the neighborhood.

Site 12. Tenth Avenue near Sherman Avenue

The next stop is just across the street, near the intersection of Tenth and Sherman Avenues.

Early antiquarians were interested in this whole area east of Tenth Avenue and explored the ruins of an old house along the Harlem River, to the north of what was then 210th Street. These ruins were all that remained of the house that Jan Dyckman built and where he lived with his second wife, Rebecca Waldron, the widow of his friend Jan Nagel. In 1719 Jacobus Dyckman inherited the house, where he continued to live until his death in 1772. On the property local collectors found some colonial artifacts, which unfortunately have long since been lost. Alexander Chenoweth, an Inwood resident who, like his contemporaries Bolton, Calver, and Finch, was an avid collector and also an engineer, discovered what he thought might be the line of an earthwork around the house, which may have been built to protect it from attack. Somewhat later, Bolton and Calver dug around the house and yard and discovered that this house, like the Teunissen house (see site 10), had been occupied by soldiers during the Revolutionary War. They found the ubiquitous bar shot, cannonballs, gun flints, and military buttons in the ruins. On the bank going down to the river, they found a midden with early Dutch and English clay pipe bowls; such food remains as oyster shells, meat bones, and bird bones; and fragments of bottles and earthenware dishes.

Site 13: Tenth Avenue and Isham Street

Continue on Tenth Avenue to the corner of Isham Street.

Here on a knoll between Ninth and Tenth Avenues and what was then 208th and 209th Streets, Calver and Bolton explored a cellar hole before the ruins of the house were destroyed by the construction of the Subway Yards. They found molten glass, charred wood, and ashes all over the place: incontrovertible evidence that the building had burned. They also found coins dating to the mid-eighteenth century; hardware, including hinges, locks, nails, and farm tools, among them a scythe; and a brass frame from a pair of eyeglasses. They realized that they had found the remains of William Dyckman's house, which the British had burned during the Revolutionary War and which Dyckman later replaced with the Dyckman Farmhouse that still stands at 204th Street and Broadway (see site 7).

If you continuing walking south to 207th Street, you can catch the 1 subway train on Tenth Avenue or the A subway train three blocks to the right, on Broadway.

The Whitestone Bridge and the Queens shoreline as seen from Clasons Point

Tour 5

The Bronx Shore with Views of Queens A Voyage through
Thousands of Years of Indian Life along the City's Coast

This tour takes you to sites associated with thousands of years
of Native American history. Along the way you will explore corners of the city that most visitors, and many lifelong New Yorkers, have never seen (fig. 5.1). The tour winds along the Bronx
shore, with stops in quiet residential areas and small city parks.
For thousands of years, the Bronx coast has been an extremely
attractive place to live, and today it still is. You will come upon
unexpectedly breathtaking views, and from several of them you
will be able to spot archaeological sites on the other side of the
East River, on the Queens shore.

You will be taking a number of buses as you explore this part
of the city. They offer a unique opportunity to explore these
largely unknown parts of ancient and modern New York. The
buses run frequently, their routes are well traveled and clearly
marked, and the rides are short.

The coastline you will see is fairly new. Although people have
lived in the New York area for at least 11,000 years, the coastline
neared its present configuration only around 3,700 years before
the present (B.P.), when rising sea levels stabilized (see fig. 1.11).
At that time, people began settling all along the nearly 600
miles of the city's shore, beginning a long and successful adaptation to a vast array of foodstuffs in tidewater New York. Es-
tuarine environments like these, which are among the richest
in the world, made it possible for hunting, fishing, and gather-
ing societies to thrive here in Woodland times (2,700–400 B.P.).
In the later centuries of the Woodland period, the residents
added farming to their economy. The environment was so varied that one seventeenth-century European colonist, Adriaen
Van der Donck, rhapsodized that he was "incompetent to describe the beauties, the grand and sublime works, wherewith
God has diversified this land." The peoples living in tidewater

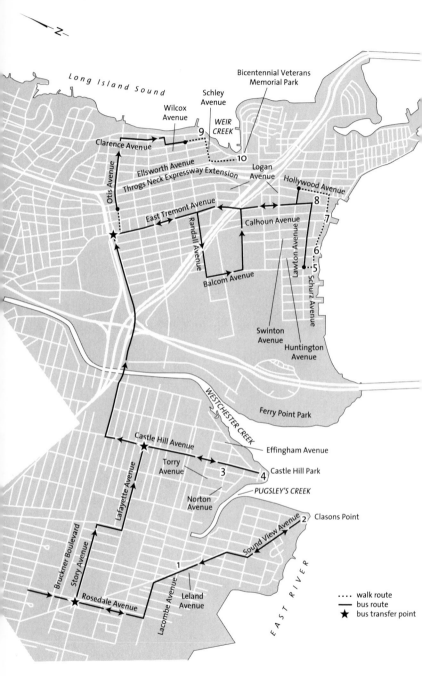

Fig. 5.1. Tour 5: the Bronx

New York during these Woodland centuries remained essentially egalitarian, so much so that Van der Donck noted, "It is not with them as it is here in Holland where the greatest, noblest, and richest live more luxuriously than a common man." Another colonist, Daniel Denton, commented that they "are extraordinarily charitable one to another, one having nothing to spare, but [they] freely impart it to [their] friends.... They share one to another, leaving themselves commonly the least share."

The area you will visit was, during the seventeenth century, part of a larger territory stretching from Hell Gate in the Bronx to Norwalk, Connecticut, that was associated with a group of Munsees often called the Siwanoy. They and the rest of the Munsees were involved in the brutal conflict known as Kieft's War (1640–45), named after the Dutch director general of that time. In 1643 Willem Kieft ordered a midnight slaughter of more than a hundred Munsee men, women, and children who were camped in New Jersey and southern Manhattan. As part of the cycle of violence that followed, there were Indian reprisals against European settlements throughout the New Amsterdam area, including the Bronx. On a moonlit night in February of the following year, the Dutch under the command of an English mercenary, John Underhill, killed somewhere between five hundred and seven hundred Siwanoy. He and his men encircled their camp and, after a skirmish, set fire to their bark houses. The Indians, according to a Dutch account, were burned alive in their homes. The exact location of that attack is not certain, although many think that it was near Pound Ridge in Westchester County, to the north of here. The repercussions of these massacres reverberated throughout the area you will visit on this tour.

These sites were dug before archaeologists with modern excavation and reporting techniques began working in the city. Some were dug by early archaeologists Reginald Pelham Bolton, Amos Oneroad, and Alanson Skinner. Others were dug in the 1930s by Ralph Solecki when he was a boy, before he went on to his renowned archaeological career at Neanderthal sites in southwestern Asia. Still others were dug in the 1930s, 1950s, and 1960s by a group of avocational archaeologists, including Edward Kaeser, Julius Lopez, and Stanley Wiesniewski, who worked on their own time, paid for their excavations out of their own pockets, and whose publications form the basis of much of what we know about the Woodland centuries in coastal New York.

Site 1. Sound View at Lacombe and Leland Avenues: Snakapins

The tour begins on Clasons Point in the Bronx. To get there, take either the 6 subway train to Morrison–Sound View Avenues or take the 2 or the 5 subway train to Simpson Street. (At the subway station, be sure to ask whether special one-day discount Metrocards are available, as the tour involves changing buses a number of times.) In either case, pick up the Bx27 bus heading toward Sound View Avenue. Along the way you will ride by our first site.

Clasons Point is a small peninsula jutting out into the East River, bounded by the Bronx River on one side and by Pugsley's Creek on the other. As you head down Sound View Avenue toward the park at the tip of the peninsula, keep your eyes open for the intersection of Sound View, Lacombe, and Leland Avenues. Today this area is marked by two- and three-story multifamily houses and small neighborhood businesses. But 400 years ago, a substantial Native American village stood here on high ground that has long since been leveled. Some archaeologists think that this village, which spread out to the south and west of this intersection, was Snakapins, a legendary seventeenth-century Native American community.

Alanson Skinner first saw traces of this site when workers were laying out Leland Avenue (fig. 5.2). He and Amos Oneroad began digging here soon after, in 1918. His hunch that this was a promising site paid off. They found more than 60 pits scattered over the area, some dug for storage, others used for trash, still others for burying both humans and dogs (fig. 5.3). Reports indicate that a local collector had first picked up hundreds of artifacts from the site, but nothing is known of them or their fate. Based on his and Oneroad's work, Skinner speculated that groups of more than three hundred people may have lived here from the late sixteenth century until the early colonial period in the seventeenth century. We can imagine a bustling community here, on high dry ground set back from the shoreline. As you will see when you get off the bus, the Native American residents had easy access to the East River and water routes

Fig. 5.2. An early twentieth-century view of the Clasons Point site, when the knoll on which it stood was being graded

connecting them with other communities throughout the tidewater area. Traces of Indian occupation went all the way down from Lacombe Avenue to the shore, where the inhabitants took advantage of the coast's rich and varied marine resources.

In the final years at this settlement, Native American families and their allies may have met here to talk of the Europeans, whose arrival brought both trading opportunities and wars. The Munsees may also have talked about the dramatic changes that were taking place in the landscape itself as a result of the European presence. We can speculate about these discussions because we know that Indian families were still living at Clasons Point after the Europeans arrived. Skinner found clear evidence of contact with the European newcomers: a beef bone mixed in among their usual household trash.

Fig. 5.3. Some of the artifacts from the Clasons Point site: (*top*) an arrowhead and (*bottom*) a pottery sherd

THE FAMILIES AT CLASONS POINT

At Clasons Point hundreds of years ago, you might have seen clusters of wigwams or longhouses for several related families, their walls covered with brightly dyed mats, with large storage pits filled with food for lean times ahead, hearths where savory stews were cooking, and probably small gardens nearby with corn, beans, and squash. You might also have seen fishing nets spread out to dry, and racks for drying meat, fish, and shellfish. Men might have been making canoes and getting their hunting equipment ready, women making pottery and clothing, dogs and children running around. During a quiet moment, you might have seen someone sipping herbal tea from a finely carved turtle-shell cup.

Clasons Point was a focus for ritual and social life. This was a place where people gathered, where smoking rituals united them with the spiritual world, where community leaders met to make important decisions, and where children were educated to become responsible adults. There were sweat lodges for men to purify themselves, small houses where women went to give birth or stay during their menstrual periods, and burial grounds for family members, friends, and guardian dogs.

We also know that this place remained sacred for Munsee peoples long after they left Clasons Point in the seventeenth century. When Skinner was digging here in the early 1900s, longtime residents told him that this had been an Indian burial ground and that the Indians who had once lived here returned annually to perform ceremonies to honor their dead. In the seventeenth century, a Dutch settler wrote of his Indian neighbors that "their burial places are preserved with a religious veneration and care," and an English colonist noted that Indian graves were visited annually and carefully tended. So what might now look like an ordinary neighborhood to some people may be a sacred ground for others.

THE CHANGING LANDSCAPE

We don't know how the bone of a cow, a European domesticated animal, wound up mingled with other more traditional Munsee household refuse here and at other sites in the city. The meat could have been given, bought, or stolen, or the livestock could have been raised by the community. Written accounts suggest all of these possibilities.

No matter how the meat got here, this seemingly insignificant find underscores the profound and irrevocable economic and ecological changes taking place not only here but throughout seventeenth-century coastal New York. As the colonial settlements grew, Dutch and English farms began expanding more and more into Munsee territory. The colonists cut down forests for lumber, cleared fields, planted European crops, and grazed European animals. These practices radically altered local ecosystems and destroyed the habitats of many of the animals that the Munsees had traditionally hunted and the plants on which they had depended.

Compounding these changes was the tense political climate in the mid-seventeenth century. Not only did the wars take energies away from economic activities, but Munsee and Dutch also destroyed each others' crops as part of the conflicts. As a result, the Munsees had to find new strategies to get food and to deal with their rapidly changing natural world, which they were now sharing with the colonists. This piece of cow bone , then, is evidence of the dramatic changes in the economy and landscape that were taking place throughout New York.

Site 2. Clasons Point Park

Get off the bus at the end of the line. Clasons Point Park is just ahead of you, fronting on the East River. There is a small yacht club here, and the park itself has benches where you may sit and enjoy the view and even watch neighborhood residents fishing for striped bass, porgies, flukes, or bluefish.

Skinner excavated several shell middens along the shore, but his only comment about them was that they seemed older to him than those near Lacombe Avenue. When Skinner was digging here, this was a popular summer resort, and day trippers would take the trolley along what is now Sound View Avenue to get to the beaches and dance halls that lined the shore. When construction workers were building the various park attractions, they unearthed several human skeletons, which were probably Native American.

Walk to the western edge of the park and look to the southwest across the river toward Queens. Locate La Guardia airport, over on the west side of Flushing Bay. During grading operations for the airport, in the 1930s, Ralph Solecki discovered a site near one of the hangars of an earlier airport that had stood there. That site is one of the few that tells us anything about the Early Woodland peoples who settled here around 2,700 to 2,000 years ago. They were among the first in the region to make pottery, and they left behind some of their broken cooking and storage pots along with all sorts of discarded and broken tools, including hunting equipment, wood- and hide-working tools, stones for grinding pigment, bone awls that could be used in basket making or for punching holes in hides for making clothing, and some bone needles (fig. 5.4). The variety of tools and their everyday functions suggest that North Beach may have been a base camp for a small family group living along the coast.

Now look to the left of the airport, over to the east side of Flushing Bay, where you can see a wooded area. Just beyond that is the College Point section of Queens. In 1861, workers excavating a sandy bluff there came upon some skeletons. Years later, in the early 1930s, Solecki discovered another burial and some pottery similar to the kind that Skinner had found at the Clasons Point site, just behind you. Additional burials were found in the College Point section of Queens when that whole area was graded and the soil taken away to use as fill for the 1939 World's Fair grounds, which Robert Moses was building in Flushing. Later, in 1954, Stanley Wiesniewski and Julius Lopez found signs of an ancient ritual when a knoll was being leveled to put in the foundations of a new building. A decapitated and de-tailed dog was found in its own grave. Placed with the dog was a fisher (a weasel-like mammal), which had also been decapitated. Along the spine someone had arranged a scallop, a clam, and an oyster. Three stones were found aligned in a row between the dog's legs. Where the dog's head would have been was the charred jaw of a dog, presumably of the same animal. The burial itself was covered with layers of ash and charcoal.

Scan the Queens shoreline further to the east, where the Whitestone Bridge (the first bridge you see) reaches the eastern side of Powell's Cove in Queens. Bolton reports that he and others identified a series of Native American shell middens, fishing stations, and residential sites all along that shoreline and the higher ground that abuts it. A Native American cemetery was found near the bridge's terminus in the 1850s. Most of these sites, and the cemetery, have long since been destroyed, and unfortunately little is known of them. Yet their existence reveals that New York's vast coastline has long been a focus of transportation, trade, and settlement.

Fig. 5.4. A drawing of a typical Early Woodland pot. Sherds from broken and discarded pots similar to this one were found in coastal New York.

When they were living at Clasons Point near Leland Avenue, the Indian residents might well have seen a neighboring settlement and fortified enclosure rising to the east, across a salt meadow and Pugsley's Creek (which you can see emptying into the East River as you look northeast from the eastern side of the park), at today's Castle Hill. But we are not sure whether the two villages were occupied at the same time.

Site 3. Castle Hill and Norton Avenues: A Munsee Castle

To reach the Castle Hill settlement, take the Bx27 bus back to Story Avenue and pick up the Bx5 bus (headed toward Bruckner Boulevard) there. Get off the bus just after it turns left from Lafayette Avenue onto Castle Hill Avenue and transfer to the Bx22 bus (marked Castle Hill Avenue; its stop is just across the street) heading south to Castle Hill Park at the shoreline.

On your way down Castle Hill Avenue, you will pass the location where a large Munsee palisaded enclosure (or "castle") and settlement is said to have stood on the crest of the hill early in the seventeenth century. The fort reportedly was in the area now bounded by Effingham and Torry Avenues and Lacombe and Norton Avenues, which Castle Hill Avenue bisects today. This hillcrest is visible from the water, as you will see at site 4, and some claim that this is the Munsee fort that the Dutch adventurer Adriaen Block saw when he sailed by in 1614–15. Although no remains of the fort itself have been found, Alanson Skinner discovered traces of a substantial eight-acre settlement spread out below Norton Avenue.

Site 4. Castle Hill Park

Get off the bus at the last stop and walk to the small park that fronts the East River.

At the entrance to the park is a plaque detailing the history of the area. If you look back up the avenue, you can see where the "castle" once stood at the crest of the hill. Here, at Castle Hill Park, you can get an idea of the different ways that various groups of people in the Woodland centuries adapted to life in tidewater New York.

Near the bottom of the avenue, not far from the park's entrance, Skinner found remnants of a Native American wampum or shell bead manufactory, probably dating to the first half of the seventeenth century (fig. 5.5). The place where these beads, so vital in trade and ritual, were made has been either destroyed by grading or deeply buried under the landfill.

If you face the river and follow the path to the right, or west, you will be able to see Clasons Point (see site 2), just on the other side of Pugsley's Creek. If you walk to the left and look east, across Westchester Creek, you'll see Ferry Point Park. There, in the mid-nineteenth century, antiquarians discovered the remains of an extensive Indian cemetery and settlement near the tip of what is now the modern park, in an area then known as Burial Point. This must have been an important sacred spot for the Munsee people, for early European settlers tell of Indians coming from a wide area to bring their dead for burial. The cemetery reportedly was on high ground above a neighboring marshland and would have been clearly visible from Castle Hill or from the point where you are standing. There are also accounts of artifacts and shell middens found scattered all along the shoreline. But both the site and the marshland fell victim to the massive development

Fig. 5.5. White wampum beads found in New York State

WAMPUM

The Europeans assumed that the purple and white shell beads commonly called wampum were Indian money. But for the Indian peoples here and in the interior, shell beads had had profound spiritual and social values long before the Europeans arrived. For many northeastern Indians, shell, like copper, had mythological origins and was associated with health and success in courtship, hunting, and war. It was related to the concept of life itself, and exchanges of wampum marked many important phases in an individual's life as well as relationships between social groups. The beads were made from shellfish found along the coast of New York and southern New England—from the central column of the whelk's shell and from the purple spot on the quahog's shell.

Europeans soon wanted wampum to use in trading for furs with the Indians in the interior, who were especially eager for it. The Dutch began demanding large amounts in tribute and then used the beads not only in the fur trade but also as exchange in treaties with the Indians. And for a while the Europeans themselves used it as money to buy not only furs and tobacco but also grains, land, and services, and even to put into church collection plates.

Native economies began to focus more and more on making this highly prized commodity that was becoming the money that ran New Amsterdam. For the Indians here, making wampum became a way of acquiring trade goods and provided them with an entrée into the European economy. The Munsees' innovative response for the need for money was quite simply to make it. And so, for a brief period in the seventeenth century, the Native peoples in coastal New York became the minters for everyone and were a vital part of the newly formed trans-Atlantic economy. Wampum was made not only at Castle Hill but also at Clasons Point (see site 2), Weir Creek (see site 9), and Ryders Pond (see tour 8, site 8).

schemes of Robert Moses. The Native American cemetery was apparently located in the area now made up largely of the approaches to the Whitestone Bridge and the Hutchinson River Parkway. As for Robert Moses, that quintessential architect of New York's modern landscape (including some of what you see here), he was, as archaeologist Ralph Solecki claimed and many others would agree, the "one man who can be blamed for more single handed destruction of archaeological sites in the New York City area" than any other person.

Site 5. Schurz Avenue at Balcom Avenue

Get back on the Bx22 bus heading up Castle Hill Avenue and pick up the Bx5 again (heading toward Bruckner Boulevard) at the intersection with Lafayette Avenue. Take the bus to East Tremont Avenue, a busy commercial street. Switch to the Bx42 and get off at the end of the line, at Balcom Avenue. Walk down one block to Schurz Avenue, to the first of a series of stops along this street. All the sites on this part of the tour are within easy walking distance of each other.

The area where you are standing is part of Throgs Neck, the peninsula that marks the western end of Long Island Sound and the eastern end of the East River. It is now a quiet residential community with beachfront condos and small one- and two-family houses. During the Woodland period, the area along this particular stretch of Schurz Avenue, between Balcom and Hollywood Avenues, was home to generations of Indian peoples for thousands of years. Then as now, its location made this an attractive place to live. It featured a nearby freshwater spring, good landing spots for canoes, and access to water routes connecting the residents with other communities in tidewater New York, such as those you saw in Queens at site 2, and communities in the interior to the west and north.

It was along these water routes and land trails that new rituals and exotic goods arrived in coastal New York during Middle Woodland times (2,000–1,000 B.P.). Archaeologist Edward Kaeser found traces of them in the 1950s, here at the western edge of Schurz Avenue near Balcom, where a community beach club then stood. The site itself extended for about 200 yards on either side of this intersection. Kaeser was digging here on weekends and holidays, as the weather permitted. He was excavating what he thought were the remains of a typical Middle Woodland settlement when he discovered something nobody has seen before or since: an eight-foot stone circle. In the refuse-filled enclosure he next found something even more exceptional—a stack of more than 150 plates of sheet mica. The closest source for sheet mica is in southeastern Pennsylvania, making it an unusual find at a site in tidewater New York, although large amounts of mica have been found in burial mounds in the midcontinent. Some archaeologists working there, using analogies based on practices of more recent Indian peoples, believe that mica plates were used ritually, as mirrors in shamanic healing and divination in funerals and other ceremonies. The mica found here may have been imported for a local religious leader to use in similar rituals and left here, by accident or design, never to be seen again until Kaeser discovered it at least a thousand years later.

Native peoples also celebrated other important rituals in coastal New York. Fragments of stone smoking pipes were found here and at other Middle and Late Woodland and more-recent Native American sites in the city. Smoking then was part of a widespread pipe ritualism, which even today is still an important part of many Native American ceremonies. Kaeser's finds suggest that the peoples here, rather than living in isolated small communities at the eastern edge of the continent, shared religious beliefs and practices with their contemporaries across eastern North America.

Site 6. Schurz Avenue and Huntington Avenue

Continue east on Schurz Avenue one block to Huntington Avenue.

In the nineteenth century this area was marked by large mansions and beautifully landscaped gardens. Among the most prominent of these was the Huntington estate. Collis Potter Huntington was a railroad tycoon and his estate, "The Homestead," was a neighborhood showplace. The mansion still stands on the next block, between Brinsmade and Swinton Avenues, and is now part of the Preston High School. In the 1920s and 1930s, the estate began to be carved up, new streets were put in, and private houses were built. Reginald Pelham Bolton excavated along this stretch of land during that construction period, salvaging what information he could from open areas.

Slightly up the block on Huntington Avenue, where you now see low-rise brick apartment buildings, Bolton discovered several Woodland burials. One was especially poignant. It was of a child, about 12 years of age, in whose grave a mourner, perhaps a grieving parent, had placed a fragment of a very large and unusual pottery vessel. The account of a seventeenth-century Dutch colonist who observed and recorded the funerals of his Indian neighbors helps us picture the ceremonies for this 12-year-old child: "Whenever an Indian departs this life, all the residents of the place assemble at the funeral. . . . Then they place as much wood around the body as will keep the earth from it. Above the . . . [grave] they place a large pile of wood, stone or earth, and around and above the same they place palisades resembling a small dwelling. . . . But when a mother has lost a child, her expressions of grief exceed all bounds, for she calls and wails whole nights over her infant, as if she really were in a state of madness."

Nearby in another pit, Bolton found what at first he thought was a collection of fish bones. When he had them analyzed, it turned out that he had found the tail vertebrae of a very small sperm whale. Whales were certainly once abundant in Long Island Sound. Perhaps a young whale entered the East River and was caught or beached here. Bolton suggested that the roasted tail of a whale may have been part of a sacrificial ceremony.

Site 7. Schurz Avenue and Calhoun Avenue

Continue three blocks east along Schurz Avenue to the intersection of Calhoun Avenue. As you walk along, keep glancing to the right to see the river, not only for the views but also to keep in mind how important the river was to the early inhabitants and their economies.

Set back from the northeast corner of Schurz and Calhoun Avenues, Bolton found an enormous fire pit, somewhere between 15 and 20 feet in diameter and 1½ feet deep, where a number of fires had once burned. He believed that this was the pit for a communal fire, kept going for long periods of time and used by all the members of a local settlement in the mid-seventeenth century to maintain the fires in their own houses or to cook for large feasts and ceremonies. Among the ashes he found some of the usual household debris, such as pottery sherds, and some clinched hand-forged nails. Bolton speculated that some wood from the house or barn of an earlier settler, John Throckmorton, after whom Throgs Neck is named, may have been used as fuel. Although the exact location of Throckmorton's house is not known, some say that it was near the shore, between the present-day Swinton and Calhoun Avenues.

Bolton's scenario—that the remains of Throckmorton's 1640s house wound up in a big communal fire—is tempting. But in the 1950s, two decades after Bolton worked here, a number of other avocational archaeologists excavated near the foot of Calhoun Avenue, and the picture became more complex. Julius Lopez looked at some of the artifacts that these later collectors recovered and wrote up their finds. He had little information on exactly where the artifacts were found, but he identified pottery from Woodland times and a variety of tools. The collectors had also discovered the foundations of a colonial house near the foot of Calhoun Avenue. Unfortunately, the excavations of the house were very limited, and it is not clear whether the building dated from the seventeenth or eighteenth century. Curiously, whoever built it recycled some Indian artifacts in its fabric. Lopez reports that the collectors found three Native American pestles, probably used for pounding corn, that had been used along with other stones for the building's foundation. The relationship between that house and the nails that Bolton found in the fire pit on the north side of the intersection is unknown.

Just as Lopez was getting ready to publish his analysis of the collectors' artifacts, he and a number of other avocational archaeologists received phone calls warning them that the area on Calhoun just above Schurz, where you are now standing, was being bulldozed. He quickly assembled a team and worked here for several days. He and his team found 13 post holes—stains in the earth that show where a post once stood. Posts can be used in all sorts of architectural features: as parts of a house, a palisade, a grave marker, and so on. Lopez writes in a postscript to his report on the earlier Calhoun Avenue discoveries that the post holes formed a pattern and that he and his team would continue to study them. Unfortunately, he died in

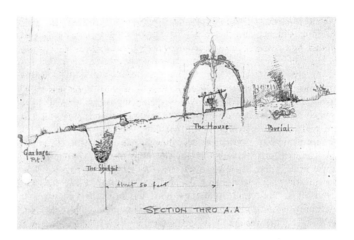

Fig. 5.6. Bolton's view of a typical Late Woodland home on Hollywood Avenue, showing in cross-section a garbage pit, a shell pit, a house, and a human burial

1961 and his work was not completed. Any other clues as to what stood here have long since been bulldozed away.

Site 8. Hollywood between Schurz and Lawton

Continue along Schurz Avenue to Hollywood Avenue. When you reach Hollywood, be sure to look to the right, where you will get a good a view of the river and shoreline. Then turn left on Hollywood and head up to Lawton Avenue.

All along Hollywood Avenue as far as Lawton Avenue, Bolton uncovered a line of fire hearths and trash pits, which he identified as part of a settlement. From the arrangements of these features, he concluded that these homes had been laid out in a clear, systematic fashion. Each house had its own stone-encircled fire hearth and its own storage and trash pits set back from the wigwam or longhouse. Near one of the homes he found a burial. Each house was aligned in a north-south fashion at right angles to the shore (fig. 5.6).

These Late Woodland peoples or their descendants may have been the ones who challenged Captain Thomas Dermer when he sailed along the shores of Throgs Neck in 1619. He described a "great multitude of Indians [who] let fly at us from the bank, but it pleased God to make us victors."

Site 9. Schley and Clarence Avenues: Weir Creek

At Lawton Avenue near East Tremont, take the Bx40 bus north to Otis Avenue. Walk two blocks east on Otis to Logan Avenue, where you can pick up the Bx8 bus (marked Tierney Place) for a short ride to Randall and Clarence Avenues. Walk south one block and you will be at the corner of Clarence and Schley Avenues.

The Weir Creek site, long a part of local lore, extended west from here over to Wilcox Avenue and then south to the area around Bicentennial Veterans Memorial Park, our next and last stop. As you walk around, you will see houses built at different times in the twentieth century and some that are brand new. This landscape looked very different both when Skinner and Oneroad were digging here in 1917 and 1918 (fig. 5.7) and when it was occupied in the 1600s (fig. 5.8).

The site is near what was once a freshwater spring at the mouth of Weir Creek. This waterway got its name from the early colonial settlers who reportedly had seen and copied the Native American practice of building reed weirs and placing them across the mouth of the creek to catch fish borne on the outgoing tide. Much of the creek was filled in during the 1950s as part of Robert Moses's transformation of the city, and the creek and parts of the site may now underlie sections of the Throgs Neck Expressway and the nearby park.

This site is especially rich in Bronx history. Weir Creek has

Fig. 5.7. The Weir Creek site in 1918, when Skinner and Oneroad were digging there

Fig. 5.8. The Weir Creek site during the Late Woodland as Bolton imagined it

been occupied on and off for at least 6,000 years. Some of its earliest occupants, the Late Archaic peoples (ca. 6,000–2,700 B.P.), left behind their distinctive spear points as well as items that were new in the area: carefully crafted stone weights popularly known as bannerstones. These stones are designed to fit on the wooden shafts of atlatls, or spear throwers. A spear thrower so weighted would be a very forceful device, which would propel the spear toward its target with a strong whiplike effect. By Late Archaic times, these powerful weapons had become a common part of the arsenal of local hunters, including those here at Weir Creek (fig. 5.9).

During their work at the site, Skinner and Oneroad also found other tools and weapons, as well as sherds from broken cooking and storage pots left behind by a number of Woodland peoples (fig. 5.10), mostly in the more northern upland section of the site. Among the finds were triangular arrowheads—signs of a new weapon, the bow and arrow, that became popular here in the Late Woodland. Arrows have a longer and more accurate range than spears, and hunters could now shoot game (or enemies, for that matter) from distances of up to 30 or 40 yards. In addition, they could shoot arrows with a rapid-fire technique, carrying a number of arrows in a quiver and quickly reloading the bow as necessary. Although there is no way to be

Fig. 5.9. A hunter throwing a spear with an atlatl, or spear-thrower

sure of the date, Skinner suggested that these finds are the remains of a brief Late Woodland occupation in the late sixteenth
century.

Skinner also argued that the Munsees returned for a short
time in the mid-seventeenth century. These last residents, he
thought, came from Clasons Point (see site 1) and stayed here
at Weir Creek briefly at the height of Kieft's War in the 1640s.
He found some burials that he thought were those of dismem-
bered individuals, casualties of the ongoing conflicts. Certainly,
as he points out, the Dutch were hunting down and killing Indians who were staying in isolated camps like Weir Creek. Because Skinner thought he had found two graves at Clasons
Point from which the bones had been removed and also found
two bundle burials here at Weir Creek, he speculated that the
Clasons Point people brought their recent dead with them
when they moved here. But as he admitted, the evidence is
circumstantial.

The seventeenth century was a period of great social up-
heaval and of movements of peoples across the landscape.
There is clear evidence that Munsees were living at Weir Creek
in those tumultuous times. Skinner and
Oneroad found a buried cache of 20 whelk
columellae, each carefully prepared up to
the final step of being sliced into white
wampum beads. Perhaps the finished beads
would have been traded for European
goods or given in tribute. For some reason,
the artisan who buried them did not come
back to claim them or finish the job. The archaeologists also found some pig bones in
the household trash. These, like the beef

Fig. 5.10. A pottery
fragment with an
effigy face found at
Weir Creek

bone found at Clasons Point and the wampum at Castle Hill Park, suggest the profound economic and environmental changes that were transforming tidewater New York at that time.

Site 10. Bicentennial Veterans Memorial Park

Walk down Schley Avenue to Ellsworth Avenue. As you go, be sure to notice the view at the foot of Wilcox Avenue, a block past Clarence. When you get to Ellsworth, you will see the entrance to the park just ahead. Take the path that skirts the water and continue along it until you have a good view of Long Island Sound. As you look north, you will see a wooded area in the distance. That vista is Pelham Bay Park, the last coastal view on this tour.

In 1643 Anne Hutchinson arrived in Siwanoy land. Banished from the Massachusetts Bay Colony because of religious differences, she established a plantation for her family and followers in an area not far from the modern Co-op City. Her settlement was known as Anne's Hoeck (Anne's Neck). The Indians saw her as an illegal occupant and tried to get her to leave, but she refused. As part of the cycle of violence during Kieft's War, Indian peoples from this area attacked her settlement and killed her and everyone else but her young daughter, who was taken hostage. The child lived with the Munsees until she was returned to the English as part of the conditions of the peace treaty of 1645, which ended the war. By that time she reportedly no longer spoke English and wanted to stay with the Munsees to whom she had become attached, as they had to her.

One of the most famous Munsees of the Siwanoy branch was Wampage, the young Munsee patriot who was said to have killed Hutchinson. Following his people's custom, he took a variant of her name as his own, and he was then known as An hoock. It was under that name that he was one of the signers of the final deed conveying all the territory that you have covered during this tour to the trustees of the freehold of Westchester on May 27, 1692 (fig. 5.11). In the years that followed, the river near Hutchinson's plantation took her name, as did the road, the Hutchinson River Parkway, that crosses the land that was home to both her and An hoock.

Wampage died sometime in the early eighteenth century.

A little more than a hundred years later, antiquarians exploring what is now Pelham Bay Park were digging in a mound near the water's edge that was popularly known as the place where An hoock was buried. When they opened this mound, they discovered "a large sized skeleton, by the side of which lay the stone axe and flint spear of the tenant of the grave." Intrigued by the reported discovery of what could be An hoock's grave, archaeologists working at the beginning of the twentieth century went back to look for more evidence of the burial of one of the best-known figures in seventeenth-century Lenapehoking. They found nothing. Much of the knoll itself had long since been carried off by the relentless coastal tides. But if the antiquarians and local legends are to be believed, Wampage was buried in a traditional way, among his people, and in his ancestral homeland. If you look north along the shoreline, over to the wooded area of Pelham Bay Park, you might just be able to catch a glimpse of where that grave was before it was destroyed.

Fig. 5.11. The mark of An hoock, also known as Wampage

To get back to the subway, catch the Bx8 bus at Throgs Neck Expressway Extension and Randall Avenue and take it to Westchester Avenue, where you can pick up the 6 subway train.

King Manor. The summer kitchen is the wing at the back of the house, on the far left.

Tour 6

The Farms and Towns of Queens County

This tour begins in the bustling east Asian community of Flushing, continues on to downtown Jamaica, and ends in Bellerose, a suburb on the city's eastern border (fig. 6.1). Along the way, we explore early farms that are now museums, where archaeologists have worked with preservation architects in deciphering their history. We visit the Bowne House in Flushing, the old Quaker community where the First Amendment has its roots; King Manor in Jamaica, home to both Rufus King, a U.S. senator who was a framer of the Constitution, and his son, John, who was a governor of the State of New York; and the Adriance Farm in Bellerose, which is now the Queens County Farm Museum. We also visit a busy shopping and administrative center in Jamaica, where archaeologists discovered the traces of the early twentieth-century homes of Italian immigrants and the hotels where travelers stayed on their trips to and from the city.

In the mid-seventeenth century, English colonists settled all three of the European towns in the part of Dutch New Netherland that is today's Borough of Queens: Newtown, Jamaica, and Flushing. Many of these settlers, who had moved across Long Island Sound from New England, were dissenters hoping to find the religious freedom in the Dutch colony that had eluded them in New England. Although New Netherland did have an official religion (Calvinism), the Dutch had a tradition of religious tolerance compared to other European countries of the time.

Most of Queens remained rural from the time of these early English settlements until the early twentieth century. An exception was the part of Newtown that lay along the East River shore, extending from the Manhattan ferry landing at Hallet's

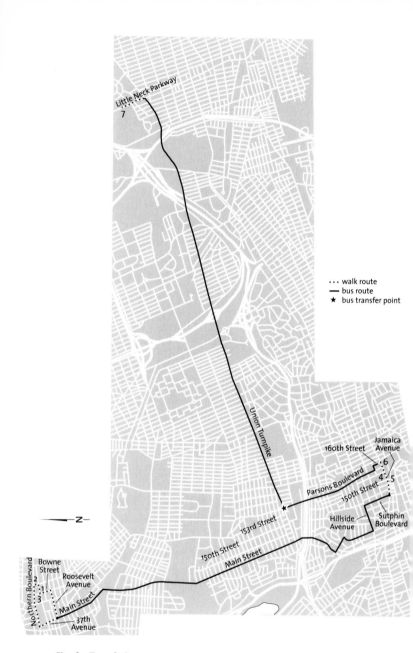

Little Neck Parkway

7

Union Turnpike

Jamaica
Avenue

160th Street

6

Parsons Boulevard

4 5

150th Street

153rd Street

Hillside
Avenue

Sutphin
Boulevard

150th Street

Main Street

N

Northern Boulevard

Bowne
Street

Roosevelt
Avenue

1
2
3

Main Street

37th
Avenue

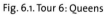

Fig. 6.1. Tour 6: Queens

Cove in today's Astoria to Newtown Creek in today's Long Island City. This waterfront area, like that of adjacent Brooklyn, began to be developed for commerce and industry in the early nineteenth century. The rest of the county was dotted with towns where farmers brought their goods for shipment to the city.

Throughout the colonial period, the county's agricultural base included the livestock and grains that farmers produced for export. But after the Erie Canal made the vast agricultural lands of the interior accessible, Queens farmers began to specialize in perishable products, such as vegetables and dairy goods, to feed the soaring populations of New York and Brooklyn.

In the mid-nineteenth century one industry did come to Queens: accommodating the dead. After New York City (which then included only Manhattan) outlawed burials within its limits in the 1850s, Brooklyn and Queens began to serve as a cemetery for New York. By the end of the century, Newtown included two thousand acres of cemetery, which held 1.5 million interments.

Site 1. 37-01 Bowne Street: The Bowne House

Take the 7 subway to its last stop, at Main Street and Roosevelt Avenue, the heart of Flushing, today a vibrant shopping center for the city's vast east Asian communities. Walk three blocks east on Roosevelt Avenue, turn left onto Bowne Street, and walk a block north through this quiet residential neighborhood lined with trees and low-rise red brick apartment buildings to 37-01 Bowne Street. There you will see the Dutch colonial Bowne House set in a small park. Call 718-359-0528 for its visiting hours and admission policy.

In 1645 Director General Willem Kieft of the Dutch West India Company gave English settlers from New England the patent to establish the town of Flushing. The setting was attractive because of its agricultural potential. Later, in the eighteenth and nineteenth centuries, the area became known for its nurseries, including the Linnaean Gardens, one of the first commercial nurseries in the country. But Flushing is particularly known for the special place it holds in the history of religious freedom in the United States. The patent that Kieft had granted included a provision guaranteeing the Flushing residents the same religious freedom that the Dutch enjoyed at home in the Netherlands.

In 1657 English Quaker missionaries arrived on Long Island and began to make converts among the English settlers there, particularly in Flushing. In the intervening decade, Peter Stuyvesant had replaced Kieft as director general, and he, unlike his predecessor and many of his countrymen, was a rigidly orthodox Calvinist. New Netherland quickly passed a law outlawing Quakers in the colony and threatened to prosecute those who took them in. After a Flushing resident was fined under this law, his neighbors came to his defense and drew up a petition, which 31 of them signed. It declared that they could not abide by the new law because it constituted a violation of the freedom of worship that had been guaranteed to the town's residents in its patent. Known as the Flushing Remonstrance, this is one of the first documents supporting religious tolerance in what is now the United States and is looked on as directly ancestral to the First Amendment. Stuyvesant, however, was not impressed, and he arrested and fined those he thought were responsible.

Five years later, in 1662, officials arrested John Bowne for holding Quaker meetings in his home—the farmhouse where you are now. After being tried in New Amsterdam, Bowne was banished from the colony. He went to the Netherlands, where he appealed to the directors of the Dutch West India Company. Always pragmatic, they supported Bowne against their own employee, Stuyvesant, because they realized that religious tolerance would appeal to potential immigrants who were dissenters, and the colony desperately needed settlers in order to survive. Bowne then returned here to his home in Flushing. The Bowne House is one of the oldest houses in New York City (fig. 6.2).

A number of archaeologists from nearby Queens College have worked with architectural preservationists at the Bowne House. Since 1997, James Moore and his students have been excavating there to help document the history of the house and its landscape. When the architects' plans call for any underground disturbance, like checking a foundation wall, Moore and his students go in first. Because they dig only in places that the architects will disturb, most of their work has been confined to

Fig. 6.2. The Bowne House. The kitchen, formerly believed to be the oldest part of the house, is the section with the porch, pillars, and chimney on the right side of the view. The dining room is just to the left of the kitchen.

the area within about three feet of the foundation wall of the house. Nevertheless, Moore has discovered some interesting features about the house and the people who lived there; in fact, some of his findings have challenged earlier interpretations of the house's history.

When Moore first started working at the house, the conventional wisdom was that the kitchen was its oldest part and was built in 1661 (see fig. 6.2). When the architects wanted to work on the foundation wall there, Moore had a chance to dig under the kitchen floor, in the builders' trench. And there he discovered that this assumption simply could not be true.

First of all, when he looked at the foundation walls, he could see that the wall that the kitchen shared with the adjacent dining room was very different from the other three that supported the kitchen: the shared wall was around six feet deep, made to accommodate a basement, while the kitchen's other foundation walls were only around four feet deep. He could also see that the kitchen's other foundation walls had been simply added on to the wall it shared with the dining room, and not the other way around. Furthermore, when he looked at the artifacts that the students were excavating from the builders'

WHEN WAS THIS HOUSE BUILT?

Although deciphering when a colonial house was built sounds like a fairly simple task, in fact it can be quite hard. Most cities did not begin to keep systematic records on individual buildings until the late nineteenth century. Sometimes a lucky researcher comes across a deed that mentions when a house was built on a property that is being sold. And early maps often show houses. But it can be difficult to tell whether the house mentioned in the deed or shown on the map is the same one that exists on roughly that same spot today. In fact, during colonial times people moved houses around—for example, some think that the original eighteenth-century Lott House in Flatlands, Brooklyn, was moved and incorporated into a new farmhouse in the early nineteenth century (see tour 8, site 9).

Preservation architects can often tell which part of a house is original and which part was added. By studying building techniques and technology (the kinds of nails used, for example), they can get a rough idea of when a house and its additions were built. And archaeologists can often help answer this question by excavating the builders' trench or cellar hole of a house, as Moore did at the Bowne House.

New York's more substantial colonial houses tended to be built in one of two ways. If there was to be no cellar under the house, builders would dig a "builders' trench" to hold the foundation wall, then lay up the wall, and finally refill the gaps around the wall with soil. If a builder was making a house with a cellar, he would first dig the cellar hole, then lay up the foundation stone wall along the inside of the walls of the cellar hole, and finally fill dirt in between the foundation and cellar-hole walls. Any artifacts that archaeologists find in the refilled builders' trench or in the fill between the foundation and cellar-hole walls can be used to help date the building. If archaeologists find pieces of creamware pottery in the trench, for example, they know that the house was built and the trench refilled sometime during or after 1762, when that kind of pottery was first made. And if they found quite a few pieces of creamware but no pieces of pearlware, they would conclude that the house was probably built between 1762 and the 1780s, when pearlware first became popular.

trench surrounding the kitchen's foundation wall, he noticed pieces of stoneware and a lot of plaster. That surprised him, because these are the kinds of artifacts that archaeologists expect to find after people have been living on a site for a while —plaster from finishing or repairing the interior walls of a house after it has already been built and stoneware from preparing food in the kitchen—and not in the builders' trench of the first structure built on a site. Finally, when one of his students, Dubravko Lazo, analyzed the ceramics and tobacco pipes from the trench, he discovered that these artifacts did not date to the seventeenth century, as they should have if the kitchen was in fact the earliest part of the house. Instead, they included sherds that dated to around the beginning of the nineteenth century—artifacts that archaeologists would expect to find in a trench that was filled in around 1810. All lines of evidence led to the same conclusion: the kitchen was built not in 1661 but a full century and a half later; it could not be the oldest part of the house. Instead, the dining room, just next to the kitchen, which had previously been thought to be an addition constructed in the 1680s, is in fact the original part of the house and may have been built as early as 1661 (see fig. 6.2). So the archaeological study of the kitchen has rewritten the architectural history of the house.

Moore thinks that this misunderstanding about the house's history might have arisen in the late nineteenth century. During the Colonial Revival in the 1890s, a time of tumultuous social change when many middle-class Americans looked to their colonial roots—either real or imagined—to reinforce their positions in a rapidly changing society, the house was turned into a museum. After a decade and a half the museum closed, and Bowne family members moved back into the building. Moore speculates that during the house's museum period, its Victorian interpreters may have "restored" the house to the way they thought it had been in the seventeenth century, making the back wing into the kitchen. Then, when the members of the family moved back in, the faux restoration took on a life of its own and was interpreted as the original core of the house. Until the archaeological work, the house's actual history was lost from memory.

In the course of his excavations, Moore made other discoveries, which he hopes to have the chance to explore: two cobble pavings, one along the western side of the house just adjacent to Bowne Street, and another to the east, to the back of the house near the garage. He also found a well, lined with dry-laid stones and covered with a thick stone slab, placed close to the house, about a third of the way along its northern side. The well had not been filled in when it was abandoned, and Moore discovered that there was still water at the bottom, about 30 feet down. He ensured that the well was preserved and kept safe from construction work, and he hopes to excavate it in the future. It probably contains objects that were accidentally dropped into it while the family used it.

While you are in the neighborhood, you have the opportunity to visit other nearby historical sites. The **Queens Historical Society (site 2),** located at the Kingsland Homestead, is just a block to the northeast of the park that abuts the Bowne House, at 143-35 37th Avenue; call 718-939-0647 or visit www.queenshistoricalsociety.org for visiting hours and admission fees. Also close by is the **Friends Meeting House (site 3).** Walk north to the next corner, Northern Boulevard, and turn left. The seventeenth-century meeting house is at 137-16 Northern Boulevard, a block and a half to the west, toward Main Street.

Site 4. 150th Street and Jamaica Avenue: The King Manor Museum

Walk back to Main Street and Roosevelt Avenue and catch the Q44 bus (marked Archer Avenue/Merrick Boulevard). The bus travels down Main Street toward Jamaica. After a trip of about 25 minutes, through a lively Asian neighborhood, past the Queens Botanical Gardens and other neighborhoods in central Queens, the bus turns east onto Hillside Avenue, then south again onto Sutphin Boulevard; get off at Sutphin Boulevard and Jamaica Avenue. Walk east on Jamaica Avenue, through a neighborhood shopping district, to 150th Street and King Park, the site of the King Manor Museum. Call 718-206-0545 for its hours and admission policy.

The origins of this charming house, set in a small park surrounded by residential, commercial, and government buildings, are veiled in mystery. Like many old houses, it was built in several episodes, and the earliest part—believed to be the central portion—probably dates to the mid-eighteenth century. By the

1770s, it belonged to Mary Reade and her husband, the Reverend Thomas Colgan. They added to the property, so that the farm grew from 16 to 66 acres, and they may also have built two additions to the house. By 1776 the Colgans had died and the property had passed to their daughter, Mary, and her husband, Christopher Smith. Smith took out a mortgage on the property with John Alsop. Then, in 1805, Alsop's son-in-law, Rufus King, satisfied the mortgage and bought the house at auction.

King was a key figure in early American history. Not only was he a framer of the Constitution (he represented Massachusetts at the Constitutional Convention), he served in other important roles as well. He was twice a U.S. senator, in both the 1790s and early in the nineteenth century, and twice ambassador to England, in the 1790s and 1820s. In 1805, when he acquired the house that now bears his name, he began to enlarge it and turn the property into an estate.

Over the years, several archaeologists, including Joel Grossman and Linda Stone, have excavated at King Manor. Like Moore at the Bowne House, they excavated as preludes to the museum's improvements to the property, such as building a fence, digging trenches for utilities or drainage, or trying to free the house from termites. And also like Moore, they made discoveries that revised the traditional history of the house. For example, note the extension at the northernmost end of the house (see the photograph at the beginning of the tour). This is a summer kitchen, designed for cooking in the summer and placed far from the house's main living quarters so that they stay cool in the hot weather. Written sources suggested that a summer kitchen was one of King's improvements to the property, and preservationists had believed that this was the summer kitchen that Rufus King had built. But Stone's work revealed that this building extension did not date to King's tenure. Instead, she discovered that the original summer kitchen had burned down and was replaced by the present, more substantial one when King's oldest son, John, and his family lived in the house in the late nineteenth century (John King was governor of New York State in the 1850s). Stone discovered the dirt floor from the first kitchen buried underneath the newer one and was able to date it with the help of the artifacts she found embedded in the floor. She also unearthed a British gambling token inscribed with the year "1793," which may have been a souvenir from Rufus King's first ambassadorship.

Site 5. 150th Street and Jamaica Avenue

Leave the park and cross Jamaica Avenue at 150th Street. Archaeologists have excavated along Jamaica Avenue on several of the blocks extending east to 160th Street, in advance of redevelopment. Stop at the southeast corner of 150th and Jamaica Avenue, by the garage.

This block, where the Queens Family Court and other government buildings now stand, is just to the west of the center of the colonial town of Jamaica, which was at the intersection of Parsons Boulevard and Jamaica Avenue. The town was first settled in 1656 by English Presbyterians who, having been persecuted as religious dissenters in Massachusetts, moved down to Dutch New Netherland. Less than a decade later, after the English takeover, a courthouse was built in Jamaica, making it the administrative center of Queens County, a position that it still holds today. Though close to the center of the colonial town, this end of the block was developed relatively late, in the mid-nineteenth century. As the arrival of the railroad in the 1830s and of the horse-drawn rail cars on Jamaica Avenue in the 1860s linked the town more and more closely with the Manhattan ferries, developers began subdividing the old farms and estates and transforming the area into a suburb. The area between Jamaica and Hillside Avenues was developed with single-family, middle-class homes, while smaller houses on smaller lots, built for the working poor, grew up south of the tracks. By the 1870s a large German community had settled here, and later in the century new immigrants began to arrive, including Jews and Italians, many of whom settled on Rockaway Road (today's 150th Street). By the end of the century, several of the town's "nuisances" were located on this block: a carriage factory, butcher shops, and a firehouse, interspersed by dwellings. Perhaps because rents were cheaper on this end of the block, immigrant and working-class families made their homes here. When archaeologist Robert Fitts of John Milner Associates excavated here in advance of the construction of the Family Court building (the gray brick building just down Jamaica Avenue from where you are now), he discovered traces of the lives of some of these immigrants who lived here in the first decade of the twentieth century.

Walk down 150th Street about half a block alongside the garage, toward Archer Avenue. Here there once stood a two-story frame house that was built around 1890 (fig. 6.3). From the beginning of the twentieth century until 1910, this house was home to a series of Italian families, including the Kalla family, who lived here from around 1900 until 1903; the Pette family, from around 1903 to 1908; and the Bounaruto family, from around 1908 until 1910. The house was torn down in the 1920s.

In what had been the yard behind this house, Fitts discovered several archaeological features associated with the Italian families who lived here. There were two large trash pits, both about 6 feet deep, and the bottom 2½ feet of a privy shaft (the construction of a foundation wall for a later building had destroyed the upper layers). All three pits had been filled with domestic trash, and the artifacts in the trash dated to roughly the same period, between around 1903 and 1907, suggesting that they were filled up at about the same time. It seemed to Fitts, then, that the Pette household was probably the source of the artifacts he had found. He realized that he could use the artifacts to explore how an Italian family like the Pettes became Americanized in the early twentieth century. He began to focus

Fig. 6.3. A detail of the Hardenbrook view of Jamaica, Long Island, in 1895, looking north. The King Manor, surrounded by trees, is on the north side of Jamaica Avenue. Pette's house is the one in the middle of the left, or west, side of the block to the south of King Manor. It is just to the north of the small church. The hotels are on the two blocks to the right of the large Dutch Reformed Church (in the center of the view).

on the history of the Pette family, and his research paid off: he discovered that Michael Pette, an immigrant who ultimately became a successful American businessman, had written an autobiography that was privately published in 1946. Fitts found and read newspaper articles about Pette and even interviewed members of his family. The stories the artifacts told, together with those told by the relatives and written records, enabled Fitts to form a complex picture of the Americanization of Michael Pette.

Site 6: Jamaica Avenue and Parsons Boulevard: Jamaica's Hotels

Walk back to the corner of Jamaica Avenue, turn right, and continue two blocks east. You will pass the gray Family Court building, 153rd Street, the old Reformed Church (now part of the Jamaica Performing Arts Center), and the red brick Social Security building; stop at the corner of Parsons Boulevard. You are now at the center of colonial Jamaica. In the nineteenth century, the area from the church to this corner, where the Social Security building is now, and the whole next block, down to 160th Street, which is covered today by the concrete shopping center, was lined with hotels (see fig. 6.3).

The accommodation of travelers played an important role in the history of Jamaica. Throughout the colonial period and into the early nineteenth century the town enjoyed the distinction of being a day's travel by stage from New York City, and inns and taverns proliferated here. With the arrival of the railroad in the 1830s, hotels became even more important to the town's economy.

Archaeologists working on the south side of Jamaica Avenue on both sides of Parsons Boulevard have discovered remains from several of the hotels that were there from the mid-nineteenth through the early twentieth centuries. Most recently, in 1998, Robert Fitts led excavations across the boulevard, on the site of the concrete shopping center you see there now. About halfway down the block, his crew found trash pits and a cesspit filled with garbage from the hotels and saloons that were on the property at the beginning of the twentieth century. Several of the hotels on the block at that time were kept by German families, including the Muellers, who opened a hotel—the William Kaiser—here around the beginning of the twentieth cen-

THE AMERICANIZATION OF MICHAEL PETTE

Fitts discovered that Michael Pette was born in 1869 in what is now the province of Isernia in the Molise section of southern Italy—a poor, rural, mountainous area. Pette immigrated to the United States in 1885, when he was seventeen. A few years later he got a job as a real estate salesman in Queens, where his ability to speak Italian served him well. He was so successful that he began to make his own investments in real estate. He soon became a naturalized citizen and a law clerk with the Queens District Attorney. In 1903, when he was a widower with three children, he moved into the house here on Rockaway Road, where he lived with his children and various family members until 1908.

As he grew wealthier, Pette became a prominent figure in the local Italian immigrant community. As a law clerk, he helped his fellow immigrants with their legal problems; he also founded a bilingual newspaper. But Pette was not only active in the local Italian community; he later served on commissions at the state level as well. As Fitts continued to find out more and more about Pette, he was fascinated by how Pette managed to assimilate into the American middle class while maintaining his Italian identity. His autobiography provided some clues about this process, but it was the artifacts that really allowed Fitts to see what was going on inside Pette's home.

A sine qua non of American middle-class home life at the turn of the century was the parlor, where people entertained. This was the room that outsiders saw, and its decor was arranged to impress them not only with the wealth and status of the household but also with its values and beliefs. A well-appointed parlor contained a fireplace with a mantel, carpets, perhaps a bay window, fancy cabinets for displaying knick-knacks, mirrors, wall decorations, and a piano. Although wealthy Italians had a room similar to the parlor, called the salotto, *which was sometimes decorated in a similar way, Fitts learned from Pette's daughter-in-law that poor families like the Pettes did not have such a room in Molise. But it seems that Pette did have one here on Rockaway Road: Fitts's crew found fragments of a mantel clock, of porcelain figur-*

ines, and of flowerpots, all of which would have been at home in any American middle-class parlor, as well as fragments of majolica tiles and a wall-mounted porcelain crucifix (fig. 6.4), which would have been unusual in an American parlor but common in an Italian one. The artifacts show that Pette was assimilated enough to have an American parlor, but it was one with, as Fitts put it, "a distinctive Italian flair."

The artifacts also showed that Pette understood the importance of "genteel" dining, that hallmark of American middle-class respectability at the time. The archaeologists found fragments from matched sets of white ironstone and white porcelain dishes, then popular among the American middle class, rather than the unmatched dishes that were the norm among the poor in southern Italy. The Pettes also had pieces from six different tea sets, which were a particularly interesting find: most Italians drank coffee, but tea was the linchpin of American middle-class entertaining. Fitts learned from the autobiography that Pette himself probably drank only coffee, but he may have bowed to the customs of his new homeland by serving tea to his friends and associates—or perhaps they drank coffee from teacups. The archaeologists also found a number of majolica dishes, which would have been appropriate for either an Italian or an American middle-class table. The food placed on the Pettes' table bespoke of American customs: beef was the most popular meat, whereas in Italy people favored pork and mutton. And the beef was mostly in the form of roasts—just as in American middle-class dinners. Fitts discovered, from both Pette's autobiography and his trash, that he drank alcohol at home—definitely an immigrant custom and not an American middle-class practice at this time, when the temperance movement was promoting national prohibition. There were liquor and beer bottles in the garbage, as well as around

Fig. 6.4. A fragment of a porcelain crucifix, found in a trash pit in the Pette backyard

85 beverage bottles that could have contained either mineral water or beer.

The artifacts related to health and hygiene were also enlightening. The high number of medicine bottles and such paraphernalia as syringes showed that the Pettes followed mainstream middle-class American healing practices, although they could have also used Italian folk remedies, which might have left few traces in the archaeological record. But curiously enough, the archaeologists found no toothbrushes in any of the pits. Bone toothbrushes are ubiquitous at middle-class American sites of this period; some archaeologists have even used their presence as a signal that the people being studied had adopted American middle-class attitudes and practices in their personal hygiene. As Fitts notes, their absence here could be simply due to chance, but it could also mean that the Pettes did not practice what their middle-class contemporaries considered to be basic dental hygiene, or that they practiced it in a different way.

As a group, the artifacts recovered from the Pette household —the day-to-day things that the family selected, used, and cherished—help us understand how this immigrant family, who lived where you are standing, gradually became "American" while maintaining ties to their Italian roots.

tury. In 1906 they changed the hotel's name to Lincoln House, and by 1908 the Muellers had sold the hotel and were gone.

Fitts discovered a dry-laid stone cesspool behind the hotel. Large and conical in shape, it was only 4½ feet in diameter at the top but ballooned out to a diameter of more than 8 feet at the bottom, and it was 12 feet deep (fig. 6.5). The cesspool obviously had the capacity to serve a large number of people. Although there was clean fill at the top of the feature, at the bottom there were around 7 feet of night soil with garbage mixed in.

All in all, Fitts and his crew found fragments from almost two hundred dishes, more than three hundred glasses, and more than three hundred alcohol bottles in the cesspool (fig. 6.6). The sheer numbers of these finds attest to the fact that they came

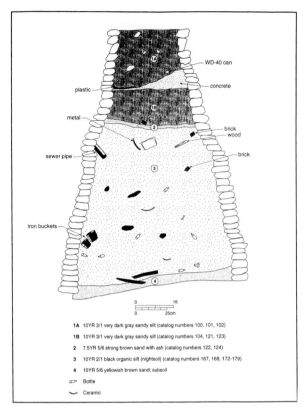

Fig. 6.5. A profile of the privy shaft found behind the William Kaiser or Lincoln House hotel

from commercial establishments. As the archaeologists dated the artifacts, they discovered that the night soil had been deposited over a period from around 1907 to 1909, ending perhaps when the Muellers sold the hotel.

The dishes for the most part were what one would expect to find in a restaurant—matching "hotel-ware" dishes made of heavy, plain, durable porcelain (fig. 6.7). There were almost 20 platters, suggesting that food was served "home style," as well as such specialized dishes as pickle dishes, which underlined the importance of condiments. But as Fitts noted, the artifacts also indicated that the hotel, in keeping with its earlier name and the ethnicity of its proprietors, had a definite German ambiance. In addition to the hotel-ware dishes, there were three delicate porcelain plates decorated with fish (fig. 6.8) and a pair of porcelain dishes in a square shape, all of which had been imported from Austria. Fitts also found fragments of two little porcelain figurines—one of a girl dressed in a Germanic peasant costume and one of a peasant holding a rabbit (fig. 6.9).

Fitts could also see a German influence when he looked at the discarded bottles from the cesspool. There were more than a hundred beer bottles, many of

Fig. 6.6. Some of the Riesling wine bottles found in the privy shaft behind the hotel

which were embossed with the name Otto Huber, and many Riesling-shaped wine bottles (see fig. 6.6). Condiment bottles had once held horseradish and mustard; both could have been used to enhance German cuisine.

The artifacts that Fitts excavated from some of the earlier hotels on this block did not show such a strong German accent, even though many of their owners were also German. Instead, it looks as though the Muellers chose to use a German theme

Fig. 6.7. A reconstructed place setting from the hotel

Fig. 6.8. Porcelain plates made in Austria with painted fish designs, from the privy shaft behind the hotel

for this hotel, which they expressed in both its early name and its decor.

Archaeologists have long been aware of Jamaica's potential for revealing its past, but Fitts's were the first, and so far the only, full-fledged excavations here. More than two decades earlier, other archaeologists conducted test excavations in the area now covered by the big red Social Security building, where other early hotels had stood, and discovered features from three of them. And in 2002 Fitts did background research on another area, a few blocks to the northeast of where you are standing, in a neighborhood where professionals and merchants had lived at the beginning of the twentieth century. In both cases, the archaeologists recommended full-scale excavations before construction destroyed the sites. But in both cases, other archaeologists, working for the government agencies overseeing the

Fig. 6.9. Porcelain figurines found in the privy shaft behind the hotel

projects, disagreed. They ruled that the finds would not be significant enough to justify the time and money that an excavation would require. Many archaeologists would contradict this assessment. But the excavations did not take place, the sites were destroyed, and any information they might have yielded about Jamaica's history is gone.

Site 7. 73-50 Little Neck Parkway: The Queens County Farm Museum

Continue east on Jamaica Avenue one block to 160th Street, turn left, and catch either the Q25 or the Q34 bus to Union Turnpike. Transfer there to the eastbound Q46 (marked Lakeville Road/Long Island Jewish Hospital); get off at Little Neck Parkway and walk north two and a half blocks to the Queens County Farm Museum. Call 718-347-3276 or visit www. queensfarm.org for its hours and admission policy.

This last stop on the tour is an especially appealing one. Spread out over 47 acres, this charming site is the only agricultural museum in the city. Here city children can see pigs, goats, sheep, and a cow, as well as geese, turkeys, ducks, and chickens, and enjoy programs about farming and rural life in Queens.

The story of this working farm begins more than 200 years ago, in 1771, when Jacob Adriance bought 78 acres of land from his brother, Elbert. The brothers were descended from Adriaen Reyerse, who emigrated to New Amsterdam in 1646 and settled in Flatbush, where Elbert and Jacob grew up a century later. They had taken up farming together on this land, which had belonged to their family since the late seventeenth century. After the purchase, Jacob and his new wife, Catherine, built the farmhouse here (fig. 6.10). The original farmhouse included the kitchen (which looks out on the driveway), the parlor, and an upstairs loft. After the Adriances died, the farm changed hands several times until the 1830s, when the Cox family bought it. They farmed the land for six decades, until the 1890s. Three decades later, the State of New York bought the land. From the 1920s until 1960, patients from neighboring Creedmoor Psychiatric Hospital worked with farm workers here, farming the land both to produce food for the hospital and for therapy. In the 1970s, the state gave the farm to the City of New York; it is now the site of a public park and the Queens County Farm Museum.

With the exception of the farmhouse, the buildings here date to the twentieth century; most of them were built during the property's Creedmoor phase.

Several archaeologists have excavated at the Queens County Farm Museum in anticipation of renovations to the property, but archaeological consultants Eugene Boesch and Arnold Pickman have done most of the work.

Walk down the driveway and stop in front of the house. Like Moore at the Bowne House and Stone at King Manor, Boesch and Pickman made a discovery here that changed what people thought about the house's history. The conventional wisdom had been that the house was reoriented at some point in its history. The idea was that when it was built, the house faced north, looking out on a farm road on the northern side of the house. At some point, the story went, the house was reoriented so that it looked out to the south, and the farm road, too, was moved to its current location, on the southern side of the house. But while digging at the farmhouse, Boesch and Pickman found the original eighteenth-century farm road right under the modern driveway where you are standing. They learned that the old road had begun as a dirt track that, over the years, became heavily rutted with use. The Adriances laid a new roadbed over it, made up of a thick cobble bedding (for good drainage and to bring it up to grade) covered by earth. The discovery

Fig. 6.10. The Adriance farmhouse at the Queens County Farm Museum

of the old farm road under the modern driveway revealed that the road had always been on the south side of the house, and that the orientation of the house had never been changed.

Walk down the driveway to the back of the house. Here, Boesch and Pickman found a buried, long-forgotten cobble-paved path leading southwest from the house toward the driveway. Continue farther down the driveway until you come to the large barn-like "performance tent," the westernmost outbuilding on the property. Before this building was erected, the archaeologists found a cistern here that was filled with beer bottles and the foundation walls of two earlier buildings, probably outbuildings from the Cox phase of the farm's history. The beer bottles suggest that farm workers might have boarded in one of the outbuildings and casually tossed their empty bottles in the abandoned cistern after they had finished drinking their beer.

When you have finished looking at the animals, walk back down Little Neck Parkway to Union Turnpike and take the westbound Q46 bus to Queens Boulevard in Kew Gardens, where you can catch the E or the F subway train.

Tour 7

The Town of Brooklyn The Third-Largest City of the
Nineteenth-Century Nation

This tour takes you through the old town of Brooklyn (fig. 7.1).
Although some of Kings County (today's Borough of Brooklyn)
remained agricultural into the early twentieth century, this part
had a very different history. By the mid-nineteenth century the
town of Brooklyn had become one of the nation's largest cities.
The tour begins in Weeksville, a charming group of wood-frame
houses that were part of a nineteenth-century African American community in today's Bedford-Stuyvesant, and continues
through several middle-class neighborhoods of the new city,
most of which are still residential today. You will see how archaeologists digging in many of these neighborhoods have explored the varieties of middle-class life in Brooklyn at the time
when it first became a suburb of New York. You will also get a
glimpse of the old Brooklyn Navy Yard, a major employer of
Brooklyn residents throughout its 150-year history, and its
cemetery.

The city of Brooklyn originated in the mid-seventeenth century as a town that grew up around a landing for ferries going
to and from New Amsterdam. The town's growth was based on
its proximity to New York, and as New York began to grow phe-
nomenally in the early nineteenth century, so did Brooklyn. The
town became even more linked to the city when Robert Fulton
introduced reliable steam-ferry service connecting the newly
named Fulton Streets of Brooklyn and New York. This new ac-
cessibility encouraged new kinds of development. First, of
course, was economic development. In colonial times, Brooklyn's primary role was to pass along Long Island produce to the
markets of New York. But in the nineteenth century, Brooklyn
became a commercial and industrial center in its own right,
though with a slightly different focus than New York. Because
real estate was cheaper in Brooklyn, industries that required

Pacific Street in Boerum Hill

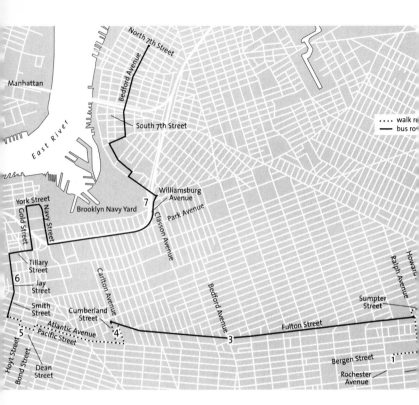

Fig. 7.1. Tour 7: the old Town of Brooklyn

space, such as breweries, shipyards (like the Brooklyn Navy Yard), ropewalks, tanneries, sugar refineries, and glassworks, tended to locate here. Brooklyn's waterfront, like that of New York, grew enormously, but it specialized in shipping bulky goods like grain so that they could bypass New York's more expensive waterfront. And as Brooklyn grew, it had to provide goods and services for its own population, such as retail stores, markets, trades of all sorts, doctors' offices, attorneys' firms, banks, and insurance companies. The strong economy attracted large numbers of immigrants, especially, in the mid-nineteenth century, from Ireland, Germany, and England. The increasing availability of inexpensive wage labor in the town of Brooklyn led to a significant decline in the number of enslaved workers here decades before slavery died out in the agricultural towns to the south.

People moved to Brooklyn for yet another reason, however: the town was only a few minutes away from New York City by ferry, and Brooklyn Heights was only a short walk from the ferry. Brooklyn Heights, along with the Village of Greenwich, became one of the first commuter suburbs in the world, as the rich merchants with businesses in downtown New York began to establish homes there in the 1820s. And as the century wore on, middle-class residential suburbs for those who commuted to downtown Brooklyn or to New York developed in the eastern part of the town.

For all these reasons, Brooklyn underwent enormous growth in the nineteenth century. In 1834 the old town of Brooklyn was incorporated into a city, and in 1839 the old grid of the village was supplemented by a new urban grid. The city's population grew to more than 250,000 people by 1860, whereas the population of the rest of Kings County was fewer than 12,500. Brooklyn had become the third-largest city in the United States, after New York and Philadelphia. It annexed New Lots in 1886; Flatbush, Gravesend, and New Utrecht in 1894; and Flatlands in 1896.

The most important event in the history of Brooklyn was the opening in 1883 of the Brooklyn Bridge, which irrevocably linked, both literally and symbolically, the two large urban centers of Brooklyn and New York. This linkage was the harbinger of Brooklyn's future. By the 1890s the city of Brooklyn was having trouble raising funds for urban services, and in 1898 Brooklyn and the other three outer boroughs (the Bronx, Queens, and Staten Island) consolidated with Manhattan into the city of Greater New York.

Archaeologists began working in what was once the town of Brooklyn after the advent of modern archaeology in the 1970s, and archaeological consultant Joan Geismar has conducted most of the projects here. Government regulations mandated the excavations of all but one of the sites we visit on this tour. The exception is our first stop: the village of Weeksville, a historic African American community located in today's Bedford-Stuyvesant.

Site 1. 1698–1708 Bergen Street: The Society for the Preservation of Weeksville and Bedford-Stuyvesant History

Take the C subway train to Ralph Avenue and Fulton Street. After leaving the station, walk south on Ralph Avenue five short blocks. Turn right on Bergen Street and walk one and a half blocks west until you arrive at the Society for the Preservation of Weeksville and Bedford-Stuyvesant History, which is on the south side of the street, between Buffalo and Rochester Avenues. For hours and admission policy, call 718-623-0600 or visit www.weeksvillesociety.org.

This charming cluster of nineteenth-century houses and yards is part of Weeksville, a free-black community founded in the 1830s (fig. 7.2). It was named after James Weeks, an African American stevedore who bought land from what had been part of the large Lefferts estate in central Brooklyn. He and other black landowners may have been motivated to buy land in part because of a new amendment to the state constitution that required men of African descent to own property worth at least $250 in order to vote, while gradually removing all property requirements for suffrage for men of European descent. This discriminatory provision remained in effect until 1870.

By the 1850s, the community had grown so large that it could host a number of African American institutions, including several churches, an orphanage, a home for the aged, and "Colored School no. 2." Some of the institutions survive to this day. A few blocks away, at 1630 Dean Street (between Troy and Schenectady), is the Bethel Tabernacle African Methodist Episcopal Church. Down Bergen Street at number 1635 (between Roches-

Fig. 7.2. The Hunterfly Road houses at Weeksville

ter and Utica) is the Berean Missionary Baptist Church; the
school continues as P.S. 243.

Faced with discrimination in the job market, many men from
Weeksville, like African Americans in New York City, worked either as laborers or in the service sector, as barbers or waiters,
and many of the women did domestic work in the nearby town
of Bedford. But perhaps because it was a separate, segregated
community, proportionately more of the people of Weeksville
were able to work in skilled trades and the professions. The village was the birthplace of Susan Smith McKinney-Steward, the
third African American woman physician in the nation and the
first in New York State.

Weeksville lost its identity as a distinct community with
the rapid urbanization that followed the opening of the Brooklyn Bridge in 1883. It later became part of Bedford-Stuyvesant,
one of the largest African American neighborhoods in the
United States. In the late 1960s, historian James Hurley and
community member William Harley rediscovered Weeksville
and founded the historical society. Joan Maynard's unceasing
efforts as director kept the society alive over the next three decades. The four houses that you see here, the centerpieces of
the society, were aligned with Hunterfly Road, an old road that
was abandoned when the new grid was superimposed on the
town of Brooklyn.

Archaeology has played an important role in the story of the Society for the Preservation of Weeksville and Bedford-Stuyvesant History. In 1968–70, Hurley and Harley, advised by archaeologist Michael Cohn of the Brooklyn Children's Museum, organized a community archaeology project, in which young people from local youth groups, including a Boy Scout troop, dug with college students and adult volunteers. Although most of the area they examined had already been heavily disturbed by demolition machinery, the project was successful as a catalyst for the community's preservation.

A decade later, Robert Schuyler and his student Roselle Henn, both at City College, ran summer archaeological field schools in Weeksville. Over the course of four seasons (1978–1981) they excavated two privies and numerous trash pits in the backyards behind the Hunterfly Road houses. Unfortunately, much of this collection was not analyzed for two decades owing to lack of funds. But as of 2004, archaeologist Joan Geismar is leading a team that is continuing with the archaeological study of Weeksville. They are finishing the analysis of the artifacts that the City College team excavated as well as conducting more excavations in preparation for construction. There is a small exhibit on the archaeology of Weeksville at New York Unearthed in lower Manhattan (see tour 2, site 1).

Site 2. MacDougal and Sumpter Streets

Walk back to Ralph Avenue, turn left, and continue back to Fulton Street. Cross Fulton Street and go to the corner of MacDougal Street, which enters Fulton Street there from the right at an acute angle. Walk up MacDougal Street, a residential street where new townhouse-style multifamily homes are interspersed with older houses. In 1995, before the modern houses were built, Joan Geismar led a team that excavated at some of these MacDougal Street properties: number 78 and, across Howard Avenue, numbers 109 and 127. As you walk down the street, note on the side of 119 MacDougal the shadow profile of the earlier building that stood at 117, with its high-pitched roof and chimney. Many of the older buildings that you pass date from the neighborhood's first development in the mid-nineteenth century. Turn left on Saratoga Avenue, left again on Sumpter Street, and continue across Howard to

Ralph Avenue. Geismar also dug where 126 Sumpter now stands.

In 1993, before going into the field, Geismar, like all archaeologists, did historical research on the properties. She discovered that before 1850 this area was farmland. Then German developers bought the land and subdivided it into urban-sized lots that they sold to their countrymen. They called their development New Brooklyn. The new owners built houses on their lots, which most proceeded to occupy. Many of the houses were frame, though a few were brick (fig. 7.3).

The German immigrants who lived here were members of the middle class. In 1860 a third of the men worked as tailors, a traditional job for German immigrants. Others worked in other crafts, such as cabinet making and masonry, and still others were saloon keepers, undertakers, and butchers. Later in the century, many of these houses were subdivided into two-family homes, and the population became more diverse: people of Irish and African descent joined the German Americans.

In the early 1990s, when the city's Department of Housing Preservation and Development began its plans for building new houses here for the city's modern middle class, the development included hundreds of building lots within a 30-block area.

Fig. 7.3. The New Brooklyn house at 109 MacDougal Street, ca. 1940

Geismar knew that she and her crew could not excavate all of them; she would have to choose. About 50 of the lots were relatively undisturbed—they all had the possibility of yielding archaeological information. But that was still more than the archaeologists could realistically excavate. So Geismar chose 14 lots for exploration: 10 of these had been occupied by long-term residents, whereas the occupants of the other four were more transient. She also chose to concentrate on backyard features—the privy shafts and cisterns that provide treasure troves for archaeologists and which have proved so helpful in revealing the details of daily life in the past.

Geismar and her crew moved into the field in September 1995 to look for features that would be destroyed by the construction. Working with a backhoe, they soon learned that only two of the yards had the stone-lined privy pits that are ubiquitous on urban sites in New York City. Although in one way this was a plus—it meant that they would finish the project early and well within budget—it was also a puzzle: Why were there so few privies?

Geismar knew that the lack of privies could not be explained by the fact that the German immigrants of New Brooklyn hooked their new houses up to the city's water and sewage system. Although records were incomplete, it seemed that the system was not in place in this neighborhood until the late 1880s, which meant that for a good 30 years most neighborhood residents had neither indoor plumbing nor the backyard privies that archaeologists consider traditional for early New York. The only explanation that seemed plausible was that most of the residents of New Brooklyn had some other means of disposing of human waste. After a lot of research, Geismar discovered a possible solution to the mystery of the missing privy shafts. Most of the site's developers and early residents came from Bavaria and Prussia, parts of Germany where people did not use permanent, deep, stone-lined shafts as outhouse receptacles, as their contemporaries in New York City did. Instead, they used the open sewers that characterized many European cities. Geismar speculates that when the new residents of New Brooklyn discovered that there were no open sewers in their new home, they may have improvised, using buckets that sat on top of the ground to catch the human waste. This practice would have left no trace in the archaeological record.

Walk back to Fulton and MacDougal Streets and catch the B25 bus going west on Fulton Street toward downtown Brooklyn. As the bus travels down Fulton Street, note the intersection at **Bedford Avenue (site 3),** about twelve blocks west of MacDougal Street. This was the site of the village of Bedford, in colonial times a wealthy Dutch agricultural community.

Location was the secret of Bedford's success. The town grew up around the crossroads formed where the road connecting the Manhattan ferry with Jamaica (roughly today's Fulton Street) intersected with the Cripplebush and Clove Roads, which led north to the towns of Bushwick and Newtown and south to Flatbush, respectively, and were roughly aligned with today's Bedford Avenue. The village, devoted to farming during the colonial period, began to become urban in the nineteenth century.

Site 4. Carlton Avenue and Cumberland and Fulton Streets: "The Hill" in Fort Greene

Get off the B25 bus at Cumberland Street and cross Fulton Street. Continue south on Cumberland Street; turn left on Atlantic Avenue and left again on Carlton Avenue, noting the rows of new three-story, three-family brick townhouse-like buildings. Note also the alley that runs behind the rows of buildings, with small back gardens, in some cases beautifully planted, and space for parking.

An archaeological study of this site—the Atlantic Terminal Urban Renewal Area (ATURA)—began in 1985, a decade before the new buildings went up here. At that time, an archaeological consulting firm conducted a historical study and recommended that no further archaeological work be done here. But in 1995, when development actually began, the archaeological community found out that looters were vandalizing the ATURA site and stealing all kinds of artifacts. Archaeologists put pressure on the Landmarks Preservation Commission, which then renegotiated with the developer, and archaeologists working for John Milner Associates did a new study of the area. This second study called for an archaeological excavation.

This part of the city of Brooklyn, known in the nineteenth century as "the Hill," is now in Fort Greene. It was first developed in the 1840s, when its streets were lined with single-family, middle-class homes, most of which were brownstone row houses built in the Italianate style. Because piped water and sewage connections became available only two decades after the block was developed, in the 1860s, it seemed likely that archaeologically rich, intact features (such as privy shafts and cisterns), like those the looters had already found nearby, were located on the properties.

In the fall of 1995, Robert Fitts and his crew moved into the field to look for archaeological remains on a dozen of the properties. Ultimately, they excavated four privy shafts and six cisterns on six of the properties—at 387, 389, and 393 Cumberland Street and at 444, 448, and 450 Carlton Avenue. In these features they found artifacts from the homes of the people who had lived here in the 1860s and early 1870s. Most of these residents were typical members of the middle class: they were American born, of European descent, and owned their own single-family homes. The men who headed these households commuted to jobs in New York City. Some were merchants, one a japanner (who created lacquer finishes for furniture), and another a lawyer. Fitts realized that studying this group was important, because this was the class whose style of living embodied the American dream from the mid-nineteenth through the mid-twentieth centuries, and relatively little was known about this group archaeologically.

Exhibiting "gentility," particularly at meals, was one of the criteria for membership in the middle class in the mid-nineteenth century. This was a time of social uncertainty for many families. Beginning in the 1830s and 1840s, a number of "how-to" books appeared advising those who aspired to middle-class status how to become genteel. The books were filled with tips on the kinds of household goods people should buy for "genteel dining" and the table manners they should use. But history does not tell us what kinds of people read these advice books, how seriously (if at all) readers took their advice, or how important it was for those readers to conform to the behavior of their neighbors. Fitts thought that he could use the artifacts from ATURA to see how people really behaved.

Fitts decided to look at the dishes and glasses that the people who lived on the ATURA site used. In looking at the artifacts, he asked three questions: Were the people of the Hill eating from their own individual dishes, as the books advised

Fig. 7.4. Dishes from one of the Cumberland Street houses, including a child's cup inscribed "Mary"

them to do, rather than from the now old-fashioned communal dishes that had been popular a century before? Were they eating from sets of matched dishes and glassware, as the new social arbiters suggested? And finally, did they have plates in a variety of sizes and serving dishes of different kinds, as the literature suggested, or did one dish serve many functions?

Fitts discovered that the middle-class residents of Fort Greene were setting up their houses just as the how-to books told them to. They were eating from individual dishes—he found many plates at each of the homes, telling him that the people who lived in the houses were following the rule of one plate for one person (fig. 7.4). He also discovered that the people who lived in the houses were using dishes and glassware that came in sets. Every household had a set of white granite (or ironstone) dishes for use at meals, and many also had sets of matching tumblers or goblets. In addition, they had sets of cups and saucers and plates in white porcelain, which they presumably used for entertaining their friends. Finally, Fitts found out that the inhabitants bought many specialized dishes as parts of these sets: in addition to plates in many sizes and the usual cups and saucers, there were soup plates, sauce dishes, cake plates, soup tureens, sugar dishes, creamers, butter dishes, pickle dishes, celery dishes, and compotes.

He looked at the dishes—both toy and real—that the Fort Greene residents bought for their children, and saw the same phenomena. He found dishes specifically made for children, in-

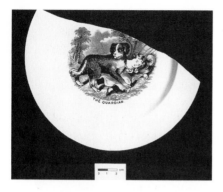

Fig. 7.5. A child's plate inscribed "The Guardian," found behind one of the Carlton Street houses

cluding mugs (there was one with "Mary" inscribed on it; see fig. 7.4) and plates (there was one with an image of a boy and his dog; fig. 7.5). Parents presumably bought these dishes to help children learn the rule that each person should use his or her own dish. He also discovered that when middle-class daughters played with their dolls and dollhouses, the dishes they used were like their mothers'. Their toy dish sets included matching plates and cups and saucers, as well as such specialized vessels as pitchers, soup tureens, and serving dishes. These little girls were learning how to reproduce "proper" dining rituals, the hallmarks of the middle-class way of life—training that would stand them in good stead in maintaining their social position when they grew up and had homes of their own.

Site 5. Hoyt and Pacific Streets: Boerum Hill

Return to Atlantic Avenue, turn right, and walk five long blocks to Bond Street. Turn left on Bond and continue to Pacific Street, then turn right. As you walk along Pacific Street, note the brownstone and brick single-family, middle-class homes built in the mid-nineteenth century. Then note the Cuyler Church (now an apartment building) at 358 Pacific Street. In the mid-twentieth century, some of the Mohawk Indians who came down to New York to build the city's skyscrapers attended this church. Its pastor learned the Mohawk language and gave a service in Mohawk every month. Finally, note the parking lot on the left and, at the Hoyt Street corner, the large brick building that extends down the whole block to Dean Street: the Bishop Mugavero Geriatric Center, built in the early 1990s in a style in keeping with the architecture of the neighborhood.

In 1990, before the nursing home and parking lot were built,

Joan Geismar did an archaeological study of the block. In look-ing at its history, she learned that in colonial times this was farmland. In the early nineteenth century, Jane Van Brunt (who was married to Samuel Gerritsen of Gravesend) inherited the property. In the 1840s the Gerritsens began to subdivide the Mugavero block. They gave two parcels to their daughters and sold the rest. The brownstone houses you see here were built in the early 1850s. Later in the century, the block lost some of its cachet when institutions were put up, including, in 1871, the Catholic Saint Mary's Female Hospital and, in 1877, the Episcopal Sheltering Arms Nursery. By the beginning of the twentieth century, most of the houses on the block had been subdivided into multifamily dwellings.

Geismar recommended that archaeological testing be done on ten of the properties where homes had stood in the nine-teenth century. Working with a backhoe, she and her crew dis-covered intact privy shafts on five of them, behind the houses that formerly stood on the site of today's parking lot, and two more behind former buildings on Hoyt Street, where the nurs-ing home now stands. As they excavated, they found many arti-facts typical of late nineteenth-century middle-class sites in Brooklyn and New York, including fragments of porcelain dolls with painted black hair and drug bottles, some with the em-bossed words "McMunn's Elixir of Opium" (fig. 7.6), which was a readily available over-the-counter drug. They also found some-thing much less common: the mandible, or jaw bone, of a hu-man male adolescent who may have been Native American. This bone was included in some fill that was put into the privy shaft at 338 Pacific Street to help fill the shaft up to grade. The fill may well have come from an old Indian burial ground that was destroyed by urban development.

Taken together, the historical records and the artifacts from the Mugavero and ATURA sites show us that the residents of Fort Greene and Boerum Hill, though both middle class, had different lifestyles. The people who lived on the Boerum Hill block in the 1850s were well-to-do, but by the 1870s many of them were not as prosperous as those who lived on the ATURA block. They rented their homes instead of owning, and more of them seem to have taken in boarders, a practice that was frowned upon by arbiters of middle-class taste. The men living here worked locally and did not commute to New York. And by

Fig. 7.6. Medicine and other bottles from the Mugavero site. The bottle on the left is embossed "Burnett's Cocoaine/Boston," and the cluster of six vials just to its right are all embossed "McMunn's Elixir of Opium."

the 1870s Boerum Hill, unlike the ATURA neighborhood, was not purely residential. The hospital and the nursery included many poor children among their inmates; there were 35 children living in the nursery in 1878 and 55 staying in the hospital's nursery in 1880. The block was hardly the homogeneous residential sanctuary, so desired by the middle class, that it had been at mid-century.

Comparing the artifacts from these two sites helps us imagine the diversity of middle-class lifestyles more than a century ago in Brooklyn, a diversity that echoes what archaeologists found in the other New York suburb of the time, Greenwich Village. In the mid-nineteenth century, most middle-class families entertained their friends at tea parties. And yet, on average, the people who lived here in Boerum Hill had fewer of the kinds of cups and saucers used at tea parties than the people who lived on "the Hill," suggesting that the Boerum Hill people either did less entertaining or, more likely, entertained in a different style.

Some of the artifacts discovered here are on view at a small exhibit, "Everyday Treasures," in the lobby of the Bishop Mugavero Geriatric Center. The center welcomes viewers to the exhibit on Tuesdays and Thursdays from 9 to 11 a.m. and 1 to 3 p.m. Call the security office in advance at 718-694-6700 to let them know you are coming. When you arrive, check in with the receptionist. The exhibit begins in the waiting area to the left of the entrance and continues around the corner to the right.

Site 6. Jay and Willoughby Streets

To begin the last leg of the tour, a long bus ride through a number of fascinating Brooklyn neighborhoods, walk to the corner of Atlantic Avenue and Smith Street (one block west of Hoyt) and catch the B61 bus heading north. This bus will take you past two archaeological sites and, finally, to the L subway train at Bedford Avenue and North Seventh Street in Williamsburg, which will take you back to Manhattan. After the bus crosses Fulton Street (four blocks from where you got on) and turns onto Jay Street, look out for One MetroTech Center, a huge gray granite building on the right between Willoughby and Johnson Streets.

This building is the centerpiece of a development that took place in the early 1990s and which encompassed seven city blocks in downtown Brooklyn. Before then, you would have seen in this neighborhood a mix of commercial and residential buildings, as well as a college and some factories devoted to light industry (fig. 7.7).

Archaeologists studying the area before the development discovered that at the beginning of the nineteenth century, the village of Brooklyn was mostly confined to Fulton Street, near the East River shore and the ferry landing almost a mile to the northwest. Although it is hard to believe, because the area is so heavily urbanized today, it was only with the enormous growth of the city of Brooklyn in the second quarter of the nineteenth century that this neighborhood was first developed. But even then this area was not part of downtown Brooklyn, which was closer to the ferry landing. It was only after 1883, with the completion of the Brooklyn Bridge and its inland access roads, that the focus of downtown Brooklyn moved inland and farther to the southeast. When this area was first developed, then, it was a residential neighborhood; before that it had been farmland.

The overwhelming dilemma that faced the archaeologists

Fig. 7.7. The MetroTech neighborhood in the 1940s

planning the MetroTech study was the sheer size of the project area—they could not excavate the whole area, so they had to choose which parcels to examine. After looking at the histories of the blocks and the properties on them, they agreed that the excavations should focus on the properties that records showed had been subject to only a single building episode and had not been disturbed by more recent development. They identified ten lots for further study, on Lawrence, Bridge, Johnson, and Duffield Streets, to the east of your bus route on Jay Street.

Will Roberts IV, working for Greenhouse Consultants, led the excavation of the MetroTech site in 1989. He and his crew located ten features in seven backyards; unfortunately two of the privies were destroyed by looters while the site was being excavated. But even without them, the site held the promise of telling us about nineteenth-century ways of life among Brooklyn's middle class. This was the first of the projects in what had been the city's extensive residential neighborhoods. Unfortunately, however, that promise was never fulfilled. Apparently because of clashes about costs between the developer and the archaeological consulting company, the project's final report was never completed.

Site 7. The Brooklyn Navy Yard

The next (and last) site you will pass on the bus is a cemetery located on the eastern side of the Brooklyn Navy Yard. As the bus continues on its meandering route, it turns right onto Tillary Street, left onto Gold Street, right onto York Street, right again onto Navy Street (which runs along the western side of the Brooklyn Navy Yard) and left onto Park Avenue. You are now traveling through the northern part of Fort Greene (the ATURA site is located to the south), where many of the people who worked in the Brooklyn Navy Yard, including a large African American community, lived in the nineteenth century. Finally, when the bus turns left on Classon Avenue and then crosses Williamsburg Avenue, look to your left, where you will catch a glimpse of the eastern side of the Brooklyn Navy Yard, where the cemetery is.

The New York Naval Shipyard, popularly known as the Brooklyn Navy Yard, opened in 1801. From the War of 1812 until the shipyard closed in 1966, it was extremely active, particularly in time of war. After the War of 1812, shipyard workers built the *Fulton*, the first steam-driven battleship, and during the Civil War they built 16 new ships and converted more than 400 civilian ships for war. Naval-yard workers also fitted out the ironclad gunship *Monitor* (which had been built farther up the river, in Greenpoint). Decades later they built the *Maine*, which so memorably sank, with 250 hands on board, in Havana harbor

—one of the events that led to the Spanish-American War. More than 18,000 people worked here during World War I, and during World War II more than 71,000 people were employed here, building and repairing battleships and aircraft carriers. After the war, however, the navy moved its shipyards down south, and the Brooklyn Navy Yard closed in 1966.

When the Department of the Navy decided to dispose of the property, it followed federal regulations and arranged for an evaluation of the cultural resources (including archaeological sites) at the shipyard. Three buildings—the commandant's house, the surgeon's house, and the Naval Hospital—are now on the National Register of Historic Places. There was a small cemetery associated with the hospital. It had been used from 1831 until 1910 for burying sailors and marines who had died either in the hospital or on board navy ships. In 1926 the navy arranged for the human remains from the cemetery to be disinterred and reburied in Cypress Hills National Cemetery, also in Brooklyn. The original archaeological study of the Navy Yard, done in the early 1990s, concluded that the cemetery did not contribute to the historical legacy of the Navy Yard because the bodies had been removed and the landscape where the cemetery was located had been changed. But the New York State archaeologist who oversaw the evaluation of the Navy Yard's archaeological potential thought that more research needed to be done on the cemetery to be sure that there was no one still buried there. In addition, some members of the city's African American community thought that the cemetery might have served as an African American burial ground and that there might still be African Americans interred there. They began to protest the cemetery's disposition. So the navy was persuaded to look at the cemetery more closely.

In the mid-1990s, Joan Geismar was hired to conduct an in-depth study of the Naval Hospital Cemetery. She discovered that although the site was not an African American burial ground per se (it was a burial ground for servicemen), some of the people who had been buried there were servicemen of African descent. Furthermore, she found a more complete list of the people buried in the hospital cemetery, which suggested that some of the burials had not been disinterred in 1926 and might still be here. She proposed two new studies to clarify the status of the burials. First, she suggested a ground penetrating radar (GPR) study of the cemetery area to see if she could identify intact burials left in the ground. She also recommended more documentary research to compare the number of those originally buried here with the number of those subsequently disinterred, to get a handle on how many burials might be left in the ground.

The GPR technique sends an electromagnetic pulse down into the ground, which then bounces back to a receiver. Depending on the density of the soil, the pulse will take more or less time to bounce back. For example, if the pulse encounters less-dense soil—as in the case of a loosely packed, refilled pit like a grave shaft—the pulse will take a longer time to bounce back than if it encounters a denser object, such as an underground sewer pipe or stone wall. Geismar, working with a geophysicist, learned that although the GPR equipment was successful at picking up burial shafts in the cemetery, it could not discriminate between grave shafts that still contained coffins and human remains and those that did not. The technique, therefore, could not tell her if the grave shafts still contained human remains.

Geismar's intensive study of historical records was more helpful. By carefully matching the names on the navy's registry of deaths between the years 1831 and 1894 (the list for subsequent years was missing) with the list of the remains moved from the cemetery and re-interred in 1926, she found a serious discrepancy: 517 people were listed as buried in the Naval Hospital Cemetery but were not recorded as having been reburied at Cypress Hills. She also learned that, probably because there was no plan of the burial plots in the cemetery, the workers disinterring the remains in the 1920s used the presence of grave markers as their guide in looking for graves. But at many of the graves, particularly the earlier ones, the grave markers were gone. Therefore, the workers probably left those unrecognized earlier burials here in the Naval Hospital Cemetery. The uncertainty about the disposition of the human remains from the cemetery was underscored in the early 1990s, when the government of Fiji requested that the body of Chief Veindovi, a Fijian who had been interred in the cemetery in 1842, be returned to his homeland.

The embassy made its request to the Cypress Hills National Cemetery, where cemetery records showed the body had been

HOW A MAN FROM FIJI CAME TO BE BURIED
AT THE BROOKLYN NAVY YARD

The Fijian man, called Chief Veindovi, who had been buried in the Brooklyn Navy Yard cemetery was the brother of the king of one of the Fiji Islands. In 1834 the chief was allegedly involved in the massacre of eight crew members from an American ship, who had landed on one of the islands to gather sea cucumbers. The Fijians were said to have consumed the dead crew. In 1840 an American expedition captured Chief Veindovi to bring him to the United States, but the ship continued at sea for two more years before returning home. By the time the ship returned, Veindovi had contracted tuberculosis. He died within a few hours of being brought to the hospital. After his death, his head was cut off and preserved in alcohol—a practice common in scientific circles in Europe and the United States in the nineteenth century when dealing with so-called exotic peoples. The rest of his remains were interred in the Navy Yard cemetery.

re-interred in 1926. But when the grave there was opened, the diggers discovered that it was empty. Perhaps Veindovi's body was never moved, or perhaps it had been moved again, as an almost illegible note in his file at the cemetery seems to indicate. In any case, his body has never been found. The disappearance of his body, the only one connected with the Navy Yard cemetery that anyone had ever searched for, underlines the uncertainty of the fate of many of the burials in the Navy Yard cemetery. As of 2004, this part of the Navy Yard has been transferred to the City of New York with a covenant protecting the cemetery. The cemetery and whatever graves remain there will be preserved in perpetuity.

The bus heads north along Bedford Avenue through Williamsburg. First is the Hasidic part of Williamsburg, just to the north of the Williamsburg Bridge. Finally the bus arrives in the part of Williamsburg that was a haven for artists and students before rents went up. It is now a fashionable neighborhood with streets lined with coffee shops and boutiques. Watch for the bus stop at North (not South, which comes first) Seventh Street, where you can catch the L subway train, which will take you across the East River to Manhattan. The subway goes west across 14th Street to Eighth Avenue, with transfers to all the north-south trains along the way.

The Gravesend Cemetery

Tour 8

Southern Brooklyn Native American and Early New York

On this tour, you will explore the early history of southern Brooklyn (fig. 8.1). You will visit a scenic spot along the coast where Native Americans lived for millennia, investigate the center of a seventeenth-century colonial town founded by an Englishwoman and her dissident followers, and explore two Dutch Colonial farmhouses, including one where archaeologists have identified what might be slave quarters.

When Henry Hudson's ship, the *Half Moon,* sailed into New York Harbor in 1609, a few members of his crew went ashore, where they met the Munsee people whose home this was. Legend has it that the place where Hudson's crew landed was on Coney Island in today's southern Brooklyn, then known as Mannahanung. Robert Juet, an officer on the *Half Moon,* recorded that fateful encounter from the European perspective: "Our men went on Land there, and saw great store of Men, Women, and Children, who gave them Tabacco. . . . So they went up into the Woods and saw . . . very goodly Oakes and some Currants." A century and a half later, a Moravian missionary working in the Ohio Valley recorded the Munsee version of that encounter as it had been passed down by their descendants, who had been moving steadily west as a result of the European invasions. They told of the day that their ancestors had gone out fishing and saw "something remarkably large . . . floating on the water." They sent runners to their people to come view this strange phenomenon. When they gathered on the shore, they concluded that it was a "large canoe or house, in which the great Mannitto [their Supreme Being] himself was, and that he probably was coming to visit them. . . . Between hope and fear, and in confusion, a dance commenced."

We know neither where that dance took place nor which group of Munsee took part in that momentous meeting. (Al-

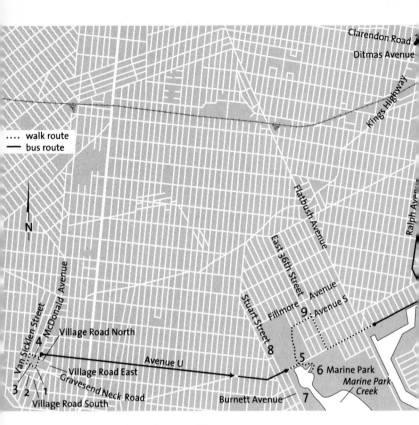

Fig. 8.1. Tour 8: southern Brooklyn

though people today tend to refer to all Brooklyn Indians as the Canarsee, they were only one of a number of autonomous groups living here in the seventeenth century.)

A half century after that fateful encounter, the Europeans had founded the six towns that ultimately made up Kings County, today's Borough of Brooklyn. The southern towns that we visit on this tour have a very different history from that of the town of Brooklyn itself, which lay to their north (see tour 7). Whereas the town of Brooklyn became one of the nation's largest cities in its own right in the nineteenth century, these southern towns remained largely agricultural until the early twentieth century. During the colonial period, farmers here grew grain and raised livestock for export. But after the opening of the Erie Canal in 1825, when the breadbasket of the eastern seaboard moved west, farmers in both Brooklyn and Queens switched to the intensive farming of vegetables, which they sent to markets in the nearby cities. In fact, as late as the 1880s, these two counties were the top two producers of vegetables in the nation. But in southern Brooklyn, unlike in Queens, Dutch Americans maintained a strong presence on the farms, and they depended heavily on the labor of enslaved African Americans into the early nineteenth century.

Over the past century, many archaeologists, amateur and professional alike, have worked at sites in southern Brooklyn. But since the late 1970s, H. Arthur Bankoff, Frederick Winter, and their students at Brooklyn College have excavated most of them.

Site 1. McDonald Avenue and Gravesend Neck Road: Lady Moody's Gravesend

To reach the first stop on this tour, take the F subway train to Avenue U and McDonald Avenue. Walk south down McDonald Avenue to the intersection of Gravesend Neck Road. You are now standing at the center of the seventeenth-century town of Gravesend. Today, this thriving Italian American community is becoming home to other immigrants as well. But more than 350 years ago, it was the center of another immigrant community, Gravesend, one of the first European settlements and the only early English one in what was to become Brooklyn.

In 1643 Director General Willem Kieft of the Dutch West India

Company granted a parcel of land that included today's Coney Island and Gravesend to the English Anabaptist Lady Deborah Moody and her followers. The Anabaptists, who held that only believers should be baptized, ardently opposed baptizing infants. These religious beliefs had led to their exile from Massachusetts, and they had been looking for a place where they could settle. This was at the time of the brutal wars between the European colonists and the Indians, and one of Kieft's wartime strategies was to give out patents for settlements to create buffer zones between the Indians and the Dutch settlement at New Amsterdam. In fact, the Anabaptist settlers were soon driven out because of Native American attack. In September 1645, when Kieft's War was over, three Munsee sachems, Seysey, Sepinto, and Ponitaranachgyne, who as children may have seen Hudson and his crew in 1609 when they landed near Coney Island, deeded the land to the West India Company, and that December Kieft re-granted the patent for the Town of Gravesend to Lady Moody and her son.

Gravesend was unusual in several ways. In addition to being the only English town in what was to become Brooklyn, the Anabaptist village was a planned community, fashioned after the settlement of New Haven, Connecticut. Gravesend's town plan expressed the Anabaptist ideal of egalitarianism (fig. 8.2). The town was laid out in four contiguous squares divided by two intersecting roads, today's Gravesend Neck Road and McDonald Avenue. Each large quadrant was originally designed to hold ten house lots arranged around land held in common. Each household was given a lot (about 23 of them were distributed during the settlement's first few years) as well as a hundred acres of farmland radiating out from the village center. These quadrants are still visible in Gravesend's modern-day grid; you are

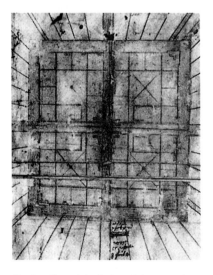

Fig. 8.2. The original plan of Gravesend

now standing in the center of Lady Moody's Utopia, and the four blocks around you are the quadrants that were laid out in the seventeenth century. These blocks are not lined up with the grid that was superimposed over the surrounding area in the nineteenth century but are relics of the seventeenth-century Anabaptist community.

Site 2. The Cemeteries on Gravesend Neck Road

Turn right and walk down the left side of Gravesend Neck Road. Stop when you come to the iron fence that encloses the Gravesend and Van Sicklen Cemeteries.

In the late 1970s Arthur Bankoff and Frederick Winter, along with their students from Brooklyn College, had the opportunity to dig in Moody's town. They knew that the original settlers of Gravesend had been English, but they also knew that later in the century they had been joined by Dutch and additional English settlers, and the archaeologists were curious to see if they could uncover differences between the lifestyles of the English and Dutch settlers. Working carefully to avoid disturbing the graves, they dug on the other side of this quadrant, in a nineteenth-century cemetery that lies beyond the Van Sicklen Cemetery. They were searching for traces of the seventeenth-century houses that they thought had once been there, along the southern edge of the quadrant. But although they found a few seventeenth-century artifacts, including some pottery and pipe stems, they found no traces of house foundations. Lady Moody's religious community, it seems, was never completely executed; some of it appears to have existed only on paper.

Walk across the street and note the house with the stone facade at **27 Gravesend Neck Road (site 3).** Some say that this house was the home of Lady Moody, but most agree that although it may be on Moody's old property, the house itself was built much later. The rumor that this was Moody's house is alleged to have been started in the 1890s by a real estate developer.

Site 4. Village Road North by P.S. 95

Continue down Gravesend Neck Road to the corner of Van Sicklen Street, turn right, and continue walking alongside P.S. 95, the Gravesend School, to the corner of Village Road

North. Then turn right again and walk halfway down the block.

The Brooklyn College team also dug here, in the northwest quadrant of Lady Moody's Gravesend, along the northern edge of the schoolyard. This part of the schoolyard was a victory garden during World War II. As the archaeologists dug, they encountered first the debris from the construction of the school's annex in the 1930s and then, underneath that, the foundation wall and cellar hole from a nineteenth-century house. Finally, when they dug around the foundation, they came upon a layer of sandy soil embedded with many clam shells, which could have been the old seventeenth-century ground surface, and perhaps part of a garden surrounding one of the seventeenth-century Gravesend homes in Lady Moody's Utopia.

If you look around, you will see that you are now standing on the south side of Lady Moody Triangle. The triangle is formed by the intersection of Brooklyn's grid and that of seventeenth-century Gravesend. Village Road North, the northern border of the Gravesend quadrants, is on the ancient grid, while Avenue U, just ahead of you, is on the modern one.

Site 5. Avenue U and the Salt Marsh Nature Center in Marine Park

Walk one very short block up McDonald Avenue to Avenue U, where you can pick up the B3 bus heading east. Get off at Avenue U and Burnett Avenue, by Marine Park. Walk east a short distance to the Salt Marsh Nature Center and look to the north, across Marine Park.

The area just outside the Nature Center looked very different in the early twentieth century (fig. 8.3). The northern part of Gerritsen Basin (also known as Ryders Pond or Ryder Pond) has since been filled in and is now part of the park, with a parking lot and playing fields. Take a look to the east (to the right if you are facing the parking lot), along Avenue U. When construction workers began grading for the road a century ago, a local resident reported that they found about a dozen burials covered with oyster shell, probably from a Native American cemetery, near what is now the eastern edge of the park. Over the years, there have been other reports of discoveries of human remains. This whole area may have been a sacred place for generations of Native peoples who buried their dead here, but most of it

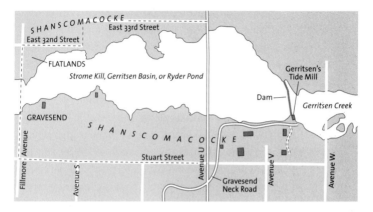

Fig. 8.3. An adaptation of an early twentieth-century map of the Marine Park area. The dashed line indicates part of the modern park's border

was probably destroyed when the neighborhood was being developed.

The Nature Center has exhibits on the salt marsh. Contact the Brooklyn Urban Park Rangers at 718-421-2021 or visit www.saltmarshalliance.org for hours and details about park walks and other events.

Site 6: The Nature Center: Looking Out over the Salt Marshes

Walk to the other side of the Nature Center and look to the south, out over today's Marine Park Creek (also known as Gerritsen Creek).

The creek is really a tidal inlet coming in from Rockaway Inlet to the south. From here, early residents—Indians and colonists alike—had easy access by boat to Sheepshead Bay, Jamaica Bay, Coney Island, and the rest of eastern Long Island as well as to Staten Island, Manhattan, and other points west. For both groups, this would have been a very attractive place to live, and there are traces of both groups throughout this area.

Although Marine Park Creek gives the impression of being relatively untouched by time, the creek is significantly different now from what it was even a hundred years ago. The plant populations of this area, like so many others on the coast, have changed considerably owing to an invasion of the reedlike *Phragmites* (see the exhibits in the Nature Center), and the effects of urbanization and industrialization have significantly affected the fish and shellfish populations.

This area used to be marshland, which once extended across coastal New York and adjacent southern New England, providing some of the richest economic opportunities in the world. In terms of available food resources, these areas could rival intensively agricultural areas in productivity. There would have been a great abundance of oysters, hard- and softshell clams, whelks, mussels, lobsters, and scallops, as well as eels, flounder, sheepshead, bluefish, and other kinds of fish. Game would have been found in the upland areas. Birds would have been plentiful: New York's coast is on the Atlantic Flyway, and millions of migrating ducks, geese, and other shore birds, attracted by the teeming marsh life, still stop over in the spring and fall during their great north-south passages.

In 1979, Bankoff and Winter and their Brooklyn College crew worked in this area as a prelude to a city landfill project that was proposed but never executed. The team discovered traces of some of the Middle and Late Woodland peoples who had lived here—pits that they had dug to dispose of their trash as they tidied up their settlements. There were fragments of broken ceramic pots (fig. 8.4) and stone tools as well as food remains, including oyster, clam, scallop, and whelk shells, and deer bones and antlers. But the team made another find that put these Indian remains and the landscape before you in a somewhat different perspective. In another pit filled with shells they also found glass bottle fragments dating to the late nineteenth and early twentieth centuries. In comparing the pits, Winter reports that oyster shells from the Native American pits were mainly large ones, almost eight inches long. By contrast, the oyster shells from the modern pit were much smaller than the ones the Native Americans had harvested. He suggests that these differences reveal the effects of overharvesting oysters and perhaps also of pollution. Modern residents note that live oysters haven't been seen there in years.

Fig. 8.4. A pottery sherd found at Marine Park

A decade and a half later, Bankoff and a new generation of students excavated here on the site of the Nature Center, before it was built in the late 1990s. They found that most of the area had already been disturbed, either by tidal action or by twentieth-century development. Unfortunately, while they were digging here, looters vandalized and destroyed some of their excavation units before they had been analyzed.

Site 7. The Salt Marsh Boardwalk: A Colonial Mill

Take the walkway on your left, or east, around the salt marsh, and then take the first right to the point overlooking the marsh and the creek.

Look across the creek to the southwest. At low tide you can see the remains of a tidewater gristmill and dam that once stood there (fig. 8.5). Gerritsen's Mill, located on the west side of the creek (the border between the colonial English town of Gravesend and the Dutch town of New Amersfoort, or Flatlands), was one of the two large mills serving the agricultural community in southern Brooklyn. The Gerritsen family had acquired this property in the early seventeenth century and owned and operated the tidal mill here. The mill continued to stand until the late 1920s, when it burned down.

When Bankoff and Winter were working here with their students, digging to the north of the mill above the high-water mark, they uncovered layers of crushed clam shells alternating with layers of sand mixed with decayed organic material. They think that these layers of crushed shell were the early "pavings" for the road that ran north along the creek.

Fig. 8.5. Gerritsen's Mill and Strome Beach as they looked in the early twentieth century

Site 8. Marine Park: The Ryders Pond Site

Return to Avenue U, cross it, and walk through the park to the northeast, heading toward Avenue S. You are now walking across what was once the pond (see fig. 8.3). Look to the left, and you will see where the Ryders Pond site once stood.

The houses to your left, the Marine Park Junior High School, and parts of the western edge of the park itself now cover much of the most important Native American site in Brooklyn. Although there are reports of other large Brooklyn sites, including one near the Brooklyn Bridge from where it is said that wagon loads of artifacts were removed, we don't know anything about them because no record was made of them at the time. That is why even the small bit we do know about what was once here is so important in understanding the city's history. The nearby area was, according to Reginald Pelham Bolton, called Shanscomacocke by its residents, and this particular spot may have been one of the principal Indian settlements in the mid-seventeenth century. It was then on high dry ground on a spit of land at the head of the creek.

Around the beginning of the twentieth century, a group of local collectors, notably D. B. Austin, worked here. Walking through the agricultural fields after farmers had plowed them, he, along with neighbors and family members, collected an enormous number of artifacts. By some accounts, they found more than nine hundred spear points and arrowheads as well as scores of other tools and potsherds. Austin reportedly also found a number of Indian graves, spaced at regular intervals of 35 feet. But there were no carefully controlled excavations, and we have no records of where they made their finds. Real estate development continued in the area, most of the creek was filled in, the park was built, and part of the site was buried and the rest destroyed; it simply became part of neighborhood lore.

A half century after these finds, two avocational archaeologists, Julius Lopez and Stanley Wiesniewski, managed to track down some of the hundreds of artifacts that Austin and his group had found. But because of the way the artifacts had been collected and the lack of any records, all they could do was catalogue the finds. Their efforts, however, showed that generations of Indian families had lived, worked, and buried their dead at this place over a period of at least 6,000 years. They were certainly here in the Late Woodland, the last great period when Indians dominated New York (from 1,000 to 400 years ago), because many of the weapons and potsherds are from that time. In fact, there may have been a substantial Late Woodland settlement here in those final years before Hudson landed near Coney Island and the Europeans settled the surrounding areas in Gravesend and Flatlands.

Native peoples were still living in this location in the seventeenth century, when colonists like Lady Moody and the Gerritsens (as well as the Lotts and the Wyckoffs, whom you will encounter later on this tour) were building their own communities in southern Brooklyn. At that time, this whole area was probably a substantial Indian settlement surrounded by gardens of maize, beans, and squash, with a burying ground nearby. Historical accounts suggest that there was once a longhouse, or multifamily dwelling, here, but no traces of it have been found (fig. 8.6). Some scholars believe that a number of related families moved here from Keshaechquereren, an important seventeenth-century settlement that was located at the intersection of today's Flatbush Avenue and Kings Highway. Tradition has it that Keshaechquereren was the main council place where Indians from this part of Long Island gathered for major meetings and religious ceremonies. Its residents fled during Kieft's War to avoid the hostilities. Many experts think that when the war was over, the Indians came here to Ryders Pond and settled with relatives and friends.

Among the hundreds of artifacts from Ryders Pond that

Fig. 8.6. A drawing of a longhouse, ca. 1650

NEW OBJECTS WITH OLD MEANINGS

The bare handful of metal weapons found at Ryders Pond gives us one of the few opportunities we have to understand the lives of the Munsees during a critical and little-understood period in the city's history. These arrowheads that Austin found in the fields were not trade items in their own right. They were carefully crafted by Indian armorers from metals they recycled from worn-out trade kettles (fig. 8.7).

Such European metal trade goods as knives, kettles, and axes were valued in part for their prestige and practicality. But in addition, the metals played an important part in traditional Native American belief systems. Native copper, for example, had been highly valued in eastern North America for

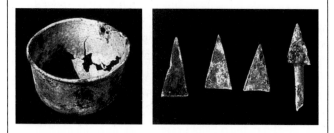

Fig. 8.7. A small brass trade kettle and triangular brass arrowheads found in the Northeast. The point on the right still has part of its wooden shaft.

Austin and his cronies found a century ago are scores of finds bearing witness to that turbulent time: European goods—rum-bottle fragments, spoons, and pipes—and arrowheads made of recycled European metals, one of iron and another of copper.

In 1665 an agreement called for this area to be fenced off to protect the Indian crops and serve as a reserve for the Native peoples. Then, in 1684, the entire Ryders Pond area west of the creek was included in a tract called Makeopaca, which was transferred to the Town of Gravesend. Three leaders, Annenges, Arrenopeah, and Mamekto, represented the Brooklyn Indians in that transaction.

thousands of years. It was said to have mythical origins, was associated with such powerful spiritual beings as horned serpents (fig. 8.8), and contributed to health and well-being.

The supernatural powers long associated with native metals were probably transferred to the newly acquired European metals they resembled. In making these points, the Munsee here at Ryders Pond and at other places in the area, including Weir Creek (see tour 5, site 9), may have been appealing to the metals' spiritual qualities, as well as to their utilitarian ones, for help in hunting and in war—both vital concerns. As for the metal spoons that Austin found, they were pierced as though they had been transformed into ornaments or talismans. Again, it may have been the spiritual quality of these metals that was important to the people who lived here at Ryders Pond.

Fig. 8.8. Lappawansoe, an eighteenth-century Delaware leader, had the image of a horned serpent tattooed on his forehead. This portrait is based on a 1735 painting by Gustavus Hesselius.

Site 9. 1940 East 36th Street: The Hendrick I. Lott House

Exit the park at Avenue S and walk east four blocks to East 36th Street. Turn left and continue down the block to the Hendrick I. Lott House, the old Dutch Colonial farmhouse at 1940 East 36th Street. Contact the Hendrick I. Lott House Preservation Association at 718-375-2681 or www.lotthouse.org for their hours and admissions policy.

The Lott House is a relic of the farm owned by members of the Lott family, one of the old Dutch families that first settled in southern Brooklyn in the mid-seventeenth century. Family members bought this Flatlands farm in 1719. The house is one of only a few Dutch Colonial farmhouses still standing in the city

NEW AMERSFOORT AND FLATLANDS

The Dutch first acquired land here in southern Brooklyn through a series of complex real estate transactions with resident Native Americans beginning in 1636. By 1647, the Dutch West India Company had granted the patent for part of this land to form the town of New Amersfoort. Unlike the planned community of English Gravesend, the town plan of Dutch New Amersfoort was similar to that of many of the other Dutch towns in New Netherland: it focused on a crossroad, in this case roughly where today's Flatbush Avenue intersects with Kings Highway. Within the next few decades, the colonists established a Dutch Reformed Church and a school, which became the focus of community life. The church was built on the site of Keshaechquereren, the seventeenth-century Indian council place whose residents may later have settled at Ryders Pond (see site 8).

Local farmers, including the Lott family, had their grain ground at Gerritsen's Mill (see site 7) and their produce transported to markets in Brooklyn and New York by wagon and water. Long after the English conquest, the town, now called Flatlands, continued to be a Dutch American farming community. The city of Brooklyn annexed the town in 1896, and along with the rest of Brooklyn, it became part of the city of New York in 1898, but it was only when automobiles became ubiquitous in the 1920s that Flatlands was integrated into the city. The farmhouses were razed and the farms replaced by block after block of two-story homes. The demographic makeup of the community changed as well: the Dutch American families were replaced by a diverse population of more-recent immigrants. In the 1920s, more than half the town's population was either foreign born or had parents who had been born overseas.

and is a potent reminder of the importance of both agriculture and the persistence of Dutch Americans in the city's history. Although much of the farm was sold off in the early twentieth century and the fields were transformed into the quiet residential neighborhood you now see, the house and about three-quarters of an acre of land remain intact. The Hendrick I. Lott House Preservation Association is currently restoring the house.

The house was built around 1800 by Hendrick I. Lott, but it was not entirely new even then. Lott apparently moved part of the family's original house (which had been built around 1720) and attached it to the new building's east end, where it forms the kitchen wing, the part closest to where you are standing. Like many of their neighbors, the family owned slaves—as many as 12 in 1803. By 1810 they owned only one. Perhaps, as family tradition holds, Lott and his wife, Mary, had become abolitionists and freed the rest. When he died in 1840, Lott left the property to his son, Johannes Lott, but his widow stayed on in the house until her death in 1853. Johannes Lott continued to farm the area until his death in 1874. After his death, family members continued to live in the house until 1989.

Arthur Bankoff and his Brooklyn College team excavated here as part of the restoration effort. Working with graduate students Alyssa Loorya and Christopher Ricciardi and Brooklyn College archaeological field schools, he dug here for several seasons, from 1998 to 2001. The team uncovered thousands of artifacts—including a gold pocket watch and a plate of false teeth—and several features illuminating the house's long history. They found the foundation walls of a separate kitchen building several feet to the east of the house, just across the picket fence from where you are standing. They also found a privy shaft around 125 feet in from the road, along the fence that forms the boundary to your right on the northern side of the property. But they could excavate only half of the privy, because the other half extended onto the next property. Excavating between the back of the house and the privy area, they uncovered the remains of several paths that led from the house to the privy and to the barns located farther to the north. Two of the paths, which dated to the late nineteenth and early twentieth centuries, were paved with brick, while a third, older path was paved with shell.

One of the most exciting discoveries made at the house was not under the ground but inside the building. Preservation architects doing a survey of the house discovered a trap door in a closet in the 1720s wing, the part of the house closest to the

SLAVERY IN RURAL BROOKLYN

For reasons that are not completely clear, Dutch American farmers, including those in Kings County, were unusual among their contemporaries in their heavy reliance on the labor of enslaved Africans, a practice that continued well into the nineteenth century. A survey of the slave holders of Kings County in 1790 suggests that about half of them were Dutch in origin. Curiously, this practice does not seem to be simply related to the fact that these farmers needed laborers to work the land: the federal census records of 1790 show that although enslaved Africans made up around one-third of the population of Kings County, where a large proportion of the farmers were Dutch, they made up less than 15 percent of neighboring Queens, a county that was equally rural and agricultural but mainly English. Most Dutch American farmers virulently opposed abolition and kept their slaves while many of their contemporaries were beginning to free them. In fact, Dutch American farmers were successful in squashing an abolition bill in the New York State Assembly in the early 1790s, and they attempted to kill the Gradual Manumission Act of 1799, which was passed in spite of them. So if, as family tradition contends, members of the Hendrick I. Lott family were abolitionists, they were unusual for a Dutch American family in rural Kings County in the first decade of the nineteenth century.

street. When they opened the door, they found the remnant of a stairway leading to the second floor. At the top of the stairs were three doorways. One opened into one of the family bedrooms. The other two, on each side of the landing, led to two smaller rooms, each about ten feet square. When the architects looked under the floorboards of each of the rooms, they discovered the remains of what appeared to be two caches, one in each room. One cache contained five corncobs, four of which seemed to be laid out in a pattern forming an X or cross (fig. 8.9), and the other included the pelvis bone of a sheep or goat and an oyster shell.

Fig. 8.9. The corncobs found under the floor in the Lott House

Loorya and Ricciardi were excited about the architects' finds. They knew that archaeologists had found similar objects under the floors and in the walls of rooms where enslaved people lived and worked in the southern United States. Those archaeologists had interpreted their finds as ritual objects with roots in West African and West Central African tradition. Loorya and Ricciardi therefore suspected that the caches might have been left here by the Lott family's slaves and that the rooms might have been where the slaves had lived. This discovery adds to a handful of cases where archaeologists found ritual objects with African influences in the New York area, showing that slaves in the North, like those in the South, had a rich ritual life that was distinctly their own.

Site 10. Clarendon Road and Ralph Avenue: The Wyckoff House Museum

Walk down East 36th Street to Avenue U, then turn left and cross Flatbush Avenue. (Or, if you prefer, you can pick up the B2 on East 36th Street going toward Kings Plaza.) After crossing Flatbush, continue on Avenue U a short distance to Kings Plaza and look for the B47 bus heading for Williamsburg. Take the B47 north along Ralph Avenue, where a bleak industrial landscape turns into a mixed commercial and residential one. Get off at Ditmas Avenue and Clarendon Road, just beyond the railroad tracks. Cross Ralph Avenue and enter the small, charming park, the home of the Wyckoff House (fig. 8.10). This Dutch Colonial house may be the oldest standing structure in the city as well as one of the earliest wooden houses left in the country. It was the first building to be designated a New York City Landmark. Contact the Wyckoff House Museum at 718-629-5400 or visit www.wyckoffassociation.org for its hours and admission policy.

The house was built by Pieter Claesen Wyckoff, who arrived in New Netherland in 1637 as an indentured servant and worked in the Albany area. In 1649 he moved to New Amersfoort. He may have built the original core of this house— today's kitchen—around 1652, although there is no actual record of the house until later, in the early eighteenth century. The house remained the center of a working farm until the nineteenth century, and members of the family continued to live here until 1901.

Several groups of archaeologists have worked here at the Wyckoff House over the past thirty years, trying to discover what its landscape was like in the seventeenth century. If you walk to the back of the house, you will see where Bert Salwen, Sarah Bridges, and Joel Klein of New York University dug in 1972, when they discovered a buried ground surface about 10 feet south of the house, just off the kitchen wing, that may date to as early as the late seventeenth and eighteenth centuries. The surface may have served as an old driveway; the archaeologists discovered what seemed to be two wagon wheel ruts, running parallel to each other about 5 feet apart, in the top part of the layer. If so, the driveway may have connected the house to Canarsie Lane, the road to Canarsie, on Jamaica Bay, that was laid out in the seventeenth century.

Later, Arthur Bankoff and his Brooklyn College field school excavated in the park for three seasons, from 1994 to 1996. They discovered what they think is the original bed of Canarsie Lane itself. Their excavations showed that this old roadbed was about 4 feet below today's ground surface and that its alignment was about 30 feet south of the house. In the late nineteenth century, Canarsie Lane was realigned. When first built, the house originally looked out over the old Canarsie Lane and the driveway that led from the lane to the farm. Then the old road to the south of the house was abandoned, and a new one was put in on the north side of the house. The orientation of the farmhouse was reversed when the road was moved: what

Fig. 8.10. The Wyckoff House in the 1990s

had once been the back of the house became its front. Intriguingly, the Brooklyn College team found the remnants of a stone wall under the original roadbed, which means that this wall had to have been built before the creation of Canarsie Lane. The wall could be the remains of a stone-enclosed paddock, a shed, or even an earlier house on the site.

Notice the relationship between the house and the surrounding city; as you see, the house is now as much as ten feet below modern-day grade. It is hard to believe that when the house was originally built, it was on a slight rise above the surrounding low-lying, marshy land. As the area became urbanized in the early twentieth century, the city added as much as ten feet of fill in the neighborhood surrounding the house as new streets were laid out and paved. The museum is planning to re-create the seventeenth-century landscape around the house.

After leaving the Wyckoff House Museum, walk a few blocks west on Clarendon Road to Kings Highway, where you can catch the B7 bus going north toward Thomas S. Boyland Street. Take it to Livonia and Saratoga Avenues, just after the turn from Lenox Road, where you can catch the 3 subway train.

Bibliographic Sources for Each Tour

Tour 1
Bearss, 1969; Boesch, 1994a, 1994b, 2002 pers. comm.; Cantwell, 2002; Cantwell and Wall, 2001; David Conlin, 2002 pers. comm.; Garman and Herbster, 1996; Garman and Russo, 1998; Griswold, 1998, 2001, 2002, 2003, 2002 pers. comm.; Richard Holmes, 2002 pers. comm.; Hunter Research, Inc., 1993; Louis Berger and Associates, 1986, 1987b; Pousson, 1986; Santone and Irish, 1997; Chuck Smythe, 2002 pers. comm.

Tour 2
Barry, 2001; Baugher, 2001; Cantwell and Wall, 2001; Dunlap 1990; EJH, 1999; Ferguson 1992; Huey, 1984; Louis Berger and Associates, 1987a; Popson, 2002; Wall, 2000.

Tour 3
Cantwell and Wall, 2001; Geismar, 1989; Grossman, 1995; Nadel, 1990.

Tour 4
Bolton, 1909, 1916, 1924; Burrows and Wallace, 1999; Calver and Bolton, 1950; Cantwell and Wall, 2001; Finch, 1909, n.d.; Jackson, 1995; Skinner, 1915, 1920; Trelease, 1960.

Tour 5
Boesch, 1996; Bolton, 1920, 1922, 1976; Cantwell and Wall, 2001; Denton, 1902; Grumet, 1981; Jameson, 1909; Lopez, 1955; Lopez and Wisniewski, 1958; McNamara, 1984; Skinner, 1919; Solecki, 1986; Trelease, 1960; Ultan, 1993; Van der Donck, 1968.

Tour 6
Fitts, 2002, 2003 pers. comm.; Fitts and Klein, 2000; Fitts, Klein, and Milne, 2000; Grossman, 1991; Historical Perspectives, 1998; John Milner Associates, Inc., 2002; James Moore, 2002 pers. comm.; Mary Anne Mrozinski, 2003 pers. comm.; Arnold Pickman, 2002 pers. comm., 2003 pers. comm.; Soil Systems, 1982, 1983; Stone, 1997, 1998, 2003 pers. comm.

Tour 7
Fitts, 1999, 2003 pers. comm.; Fitts and Yamin, 1996; Geismar, 1990, 1992, 1993, 1996a, 1996b, 1999, 2003 pers. comm.; Jackson, 1995; Ment, 1979; Ment and Donovan, 1980; Michael Papalardo, 2003 pers. comm.; Roberts, 1993; Rothschild and Dublin, 1985.

Tour 8

Bankoff, 2002 pers. comm., 2003 pers. comm.; Bankoff, Ricciardi, and Loorya, 1998, 2001, n.d.; Bolton, 1920, 1922; Burrows and Wallace, 1999; Cantwell and Wall, 2001; Danckaerts, 1941; Grumet, 1981, 1986; Heckewelder, 1841, 1876; Jackson, 1995; Lindner and Zacharias, 1999; Loorya, 1996, 2001 pers. comm., 2002 pers. comm., 2003 pers. comm.; Lopez and Wisniewski, 1978a, 1978b; Ment, 1979; Pickman, 2000; Christopher Ricciardi, 2001 pers. comm., 2002 pers. comm., 2003 pers. comm.; Ricciardi, Loorya, and Smale, 2000; Salwen, Bridges, and Klein, 1974; Sean Sawyer, 2002 pers. comm.; Staples, 2001; Van Wyck, 1924; White, 1991; White and Willensky, 1978; Winter, 1981.

Bibliography

Bankoff, H. Arthur, Christopher Ricciardi, and Alyssa Loorya. 1998. Gerritsen's Creek: 1997 Archaeological Field Excavations. Report submitted to the Historic House Trust, Division of the New York City Parks and Recreation, Marine Park.

———. 2001. Remembering Africa under the Eaves. *Archaeology* 54 (3): 36–40.

———. n.d. Pieter Claesen Wyckoff House. http://depthome.brooklyn.cuny.edu/anthro/dept/wyckoff.htm.

Barry, Dan. 2001. Manhattan Past, Queens Present: City Hall Artifacts Are Returned from Obscurity. *New York Times,* July 16.

Baugher, Sherene. 2001. Visible Charity: The Archaeology, Material Culture, and Landscape Design of New York City's Municipal Almshouse Complex, 1736–1797. *International Journal of Historical Archaeology* 5 (2): 175–202.

Bearss, Edwin C. 1969. *The Ferryboat Ellis Island: Transport to Hope.* Office of Archaeology and Historic Preservation, National Park Service, U.S. Department of the Interior.

Berger, Louis. *See* Louis Berger and Associates.

Boesch, Eugene J. 1994a. Ellis Island Bridge and Access Alternatives: Statue of Liberty National Monument and Ellis Island, Final Assessment of Terrestrial Archeological Sensitivity Report. Prepared for Malcolm Pirnie, Inc. Report submitted to the National Park Service.

———. 1994b. Ellis Island Bridge and Access Alternatives: Statue of Liberty National Monument and Ellis Island, Final Assessment of Marine Archeological Sensitivity Report. Prepared for Malcolm Pirnie, Inc. Report submitted to the National Park Service.

———. 1996. Archaeological Evaluation and Sensitivity Assessment of the Prehistoric and Contact Period Aboriginal History of the Bronx, New York. Report of the New York City Landmarks Preservation Commission.

Bolton, Reginald P. 1909. The Indians of Washington Heights. In *The Indians of Greater New York and the Lower Hudson.* Anthropological Papers of the American Museum of Natural History 3: 77–109. American Museum of Natural History, New York.

———. 1916. *Relics of the Revolution.* Privately published, New York.

———. 1920. *New York City in Indian Possession.* Indian Notes and Monographs 2, no. 7. Museum of the American Indian, Heye Foundation, New York.

———. 1922. *Indian Paths of the Great Metropolis.* Indian Notes and

Monographs, Miscellaneous Series 23. Museum of the American Indian, Heye Foundation, New York.

———. 1924. *Washington Heights, Manhattan, Its Eventful Past.* Dyckman Institute, New York.

———. 1934. *Indian Life of Long Ago in the City of New York.* Bolton Books, New York.

———. 1976. An Indian Settlement at Throg's Neck. *Indian Notes* 11: 111–25.

Burrows, Edwin G., and Mike Wallace. 1999. *Gotham: A History of New York to 1898.* Oxford University Press, New York.

Calver, William L., and Reginald Pelham Bolton. 1950. *History Written with Pick and Shovel.* New-York Historical Society, New York.

Cantwell, Anne-Marie. 2002. "Who Knows the Power of His Bones?": Repatriation Redux. In *Ethics and Anthropology: Facing Future Issues in Human Biology, Globalism, and Cultural Property,* ed. A.-M. Cantwell, E. Friedlander, and M. Tramm. Annals of the New York Academy of Sciences, pp. 79–119.

Cantwell, Anne-Marie, and Diana diZerega Wall. 2001. *Unearthing Gotham: The Archaeology of New York City.* Yale University Press, New Haven.

Danckaerts, Jasper. 1941. *Journal of Jasper Danckaerts, 1679–1680,* ed. B. James and J. Jameson. Barnes and Noble, New York.

Denton, Daniel. 1902. *A Brief History of New York Formerly Called New Netherlands.* Burrows Brothers, Cleveland.

Dunlap, David W. 1990. A Taste of the Past to Emend a Builder's Blunder. *New York Times,* May 6.

Edwards, R., and K. Emery. 1977. Man on the Continental Shelf. In *Amerinds and Their Paleoenvironments in Northeastern North America,* ed. W. Newman and B. Salwen. Annals of the New York Academy of Sciences 288.

EJH. 1999. Cover Up at City Hall? *Archaeology,* September–October.

Ferguson, Leland. 1992. *Uncommon Ground: Archaeology and Early African America.* Smithsonian Institution Press, Washington, D.C.

Finch, James. 1909. Aboriginal Remains on Manhattan Island. *Anthropological Papers of the American Museum of Natural History* 3: 65–73.

———. n.d. Notes on the Manhattan Indians. Manuscript on file at the American Museum of Natural History.

Fitts, Robert K. 1999. The Archaeology of Middle-Class Domesticity and Gentility in Victorian Brooklyn. *Historical Archaeology* 33 (1): 39–62.

———. 2002. Becoming American: The Archaeology of an Italian Immigrant. *Historical Archaeology* 36 (2): 1–17.

Fitts, Robert K., and Joel I. Klein. 2000. Phase II and III Archaeological Investigations at One Jamaica Center, Block 10100, Jamaica, Queens County, NY. By John Milner Associates, Inc., for Mattone Group, Jamaica Co., LIC, and Washington Square Partners. Report on file with the New York City Landmarks Preservation Commission.

Fitts, Robert K., Joel I. Klein, and Claudia Milne. 2000. Immigrant Life in Turn-of-the-Century Jamaica, Queens: Stage II and III Archeological

Investigations at the Proposed Queens Family Court and Families Court Agencies Facility, Blocks 10092 and 10093 (Former Block 10097), Jamaica, Queens County, New York. Report on file with the New York City Landmarks Preservation Commission.

Fitts, Robert, and Rebecca Yamin. 1996. The Archaeology of Domesticity in Victorian Brooklyn: Exploratory Testing and Data Recovery at Block 2006 of the Atlantic Terminal Urban Renewal Area, Brooklyn, New York. Report submitted to the Atlantic Housing Corporation by John Milner Associates, Inc., New York.

Garman, James C., and Holly Herbster. 1996. Phase IA Archaeological Assessment of the Governors Island National Historic Landmark District, Governors Island, New York. Report submitted to ABB Environmental Services, Inc., and submitted to the U.S. Coast Guard by the Public Archaeology Laboratory, Inc., Pawtucket, R.I.

Garman, James C., and Paul A. Russo. 1998. Phase II Evaluation of Six Archaeological Sites in the Governors Island National Historic Landmark District, Governors Island, New York. Report submitted to HRP Associates, Inc., and USCG/CEU Providence by the Public Archaeology Laboratory, Inc., Pawtucket, R.I.

Geismar, Joan H. 1989. History and Archaeology of the Greenwich Mews Site, Greenwich Village, New York. Report on file with the New York City Landmarks Preservation Commission.

———. 1990. Archaeological Assessment of the Proposed Bishop Mugavero Geriatric Center Site, Block 189, Brooklyn. For the Catholic Medical Center of Brooklyn and Queens. Report on file with the New York City Landmarks Preservation Commission.

———. 1992. Teacups and Opium: The Bishop Mugavero Geriatric Center Archaeological Field Report. CEQR no. 90-223K. For the Catholic Medical Center of Brooklyn and Queens. Report on file with the New York City Landmarks Preservation Commission.

———. 1993. Documentary Study of the Saratoga Square Urban Renewal Area, Brooklyn, New York. Submitted to the New York City Department of Housing and Urban Development by Tams Consultants, Inc. Report on file with the New York City Landmarks Preservation Commission.

———. 1996a. Saratoga Square Urban Renewal Area (SSQURA), 127 and 109 MacDougal Street (Block 1525, lots 40 and 49), 78 MacDougal (Block 1531, lot 15), and 126 Sumpter Street (Block 1524, lot 43), Brooklyn, New York—Data Recovery. Submitted to the New York City Department of Housing Preservation and Development. Report on file with the New York City Landmarks Preservation Commission.

———. 1996b. Archaeological Evaluation: (Stage 1A Documentary Study) Former Naval Station (NAVSTA) New York, Navy Yard Annex Site, Brooklyn, New York. Submitted to the U.S. Department of the Navy, Northern Division, Naval Facilities Engineering Command. Report on file with the New York City Landmarks Preservation Commission.

———. 1999. State of the Research: Naval Hospital Cemetery Historical Documentation, Naval Station Brooklyn, New York. Submitted to the

U.S. Department of the Navy, Northern Division, Naval Facilities Engineering Command. Report on file with the New York City Landmarks Preservation Commission.

Griswold, William A. 1998. Liberty Island: Archaeological Overviews and Assessment: Statue of Liberty/Ellis Island National Monument, New York, New York. Archaeology Branch, Northeast Cultural Resources Center, Northeast Region, National Park Service, U.S. Department of the Interior, Lowell, Mass.

———. 2001. The Archaeology of Military Politics: The Case of Castle Clinton. *Historical Archaeology* 35 (4): 105–17.

———, ed. 2002. Archeology of a Prehistoric Shell Midden, Statue of Liberty National Monument, New York, New York. Archeology Branch, Northeast Region, National Park Service, U.S. Department of the Interior, Lowell, Mass.

———, ed. 2003. The Ground Beneath Her Feet: The Archaeology of Liberty Island, Statue of Liberty National Monument, New York, New York. Occasional Publications in Field Archeology 3. Archaeology Group, Northeast Region, National Park Service, U.S. Department of the Interior, Lowell, Mass.

Grossman, Joel W. 1991. Archaeological Tests and Artifact Analysis Results from Rufus King Park, Jamaica, Queens, New York. Report prepared for Land-Site Contracting Corporation.

———. 1995. The Archaeology of Civil War Era Water Control Systems on the Lower East Side of Manhattan, New York. Report on file with the New York City Landmarks Preservation Commission.

Grumet, Robert S. 1981. *Native American Place Names in New York City*. Museum of the City of New York, New York.

———. 1986. *New World Encounters: Jasper Danckaert's View of Indian Life in 17th-Century Brooklyn*. Brooklyn Historical Society, Brooklyn.

Haviland, William A., and Marjory Power. 1994. *The Original Vermonters: Native Inhabitants, Past and Present*. Second edition. University Press of New England, Hanover, N.H.

Heckewelder, John. 1841. Indian Tradition of the First Arrival of the Dutch at Manhattan Island, 1811–1859. *Collections of the New-York Historical Society*, 2nd ser., 1: 69–74.

———. 1876. *History, Manners, and Customs of the Indian Nations Who Once Inhabited Pennsylvania and the Neighboring States*. Historical Society of Pennsylvania, Philadelphia.

Historical Perspectives. 1998. One Jamaica Center, 97 DME 002, Archer Ave. and Jamaica Ave., Queens, NY. The Mattone Group. Phase 1A Archaeological Study. For Philip Habib and Associates, Inc. Report on file with the New York City Landmarks Preservation Commission.

Huey, Paul R. 1984. Old Slip and Cruger's Wharf at New York: An Archaeological Perspective of the Colonial American Waterfront. *Historical Archaeology* 18 (1): 15–37.

Hunter Research, Inc. 1993. Archaeological Investigations in Connection with the New Wall of Honor, Ellis Island, City of New York, New York

County, New York. Report prepared for the Statue of Liberty–Ellis Island Foundation.

Jackson, Kenneth, ed. 1995. *The Encyclopedia of New York City.* Yale University Press, New Haven.

Jameson, J. Franklin, ed. 1909. *Narratives of New Netherland, 1609–1664.* Charles Scribner's Sons, New York.

John Milner Associates, Inc. 2002. Phase 1A Archaeological Documentary Investigation, Jamaica Mid-Block Development Project, Jamaica, Queens County, NY. Report prepared for Edwards and Kelcey Engineers, Inc.

Linder, Marc, and Lawrence S. Zacharias. 1999. *Of Cabbages and Kings County: Agriculture and the Formation of Modern Brooklyn.* University of Iowa Press, Iowa City.

Loorya, Alyssa. 1996. Gerritsen's Creek and Mill. Manuscript on file with the Brooklyn College Archaeological Research Center, Department of Anthropology, Brooklyn College.

Lopez, Julius. 1955. Preliminary Report on the Schurz Site (Throgs Neck, Bronx County, New York). *Nassau Archaeological Society Bulletin* 1: 6–16.

Lopez, Julius, and Stanley Wisniewski. 1958. Discovery of a Possible Ceremonial Dog Burial in the City of Greater New York. *Bulletin of the Archeological Society of Connecticut* 29: 14–16.

———. 1978a. The Ryders Pond Site, Kings County, New York. In *Coastal Archaeology Reader,* ed. G. Stone. Suffolk County Archaeological Association, Stony Brook, N.Y.

———. 1978b. The Ryders Pond Site II. In *Coastal Archaeology Reader,* ed. G. Stone. Suffolk County Archaeological Association, Stony Brook, N.Y.

Louis Berger and Associates. 1986. Archaeological Assessment of the Proposed Guest House Site, Third Coast Guard District, Governors Island, New York. Report submitted to the Planning Office, Third Coast Guard District, Governors Island, New York.

———. 1987a. Druggists, Craftsmen, and Merchants of Pearl and Water Streets, New York: The Barclays Bank Site. Report on file with the New York City Landmarks Preservation Commission.

———. 1987b. Phase IB Archaeological Survey for a Proposed Utility Trench, Governors Island, New York. Report prepared for the United States Coast Guard.

McNamara, John. 1984. *History in Asphalt: The Origin of Bronx Street and Place Names.* Bronx Historical Society, New York.

Ment, David. 1979. *The Shaping of a City: A Brief History of Brooklyn.* Brooklyn Rediscovery, New York.

Ment, David, and Mary S. Donovan. 1980. *The People of Brooklyn: A History of Two Neighborhoods.* Brooklyn Rediscovery, New York.

Milner, John. *See* John Milner Associates, Inc.

Nadel, Stanley. 1990. *Little Germany: Ethnicity, Religion, and Class in New York City, 1845–1880.* University of Illinois Press, Urbana, Ill.

Pickman, Arnold. 2000. Cultural Resources Baseline Study, Jamaica Bay

Ecosystem Restoration Project Kings, Queens, and Nassau Counties, New York. Report Submitted to Panamerican Consultants, Inc.

Popson, Colleen P. 2002. The House That Tweed Built. *Archaeology,* July–August.

Pousson, John F. 1986. An Overview Assessment of Archeological Resources on Ellis Island, Statue of Liberty National Monument, New York. STLI Pkg. no. 107-43. U.S. Department of the Interior, National Park Service, Denver Service Center, Eastern Team, Rockville, Mass.

Ricciardi, Christopher, Alyssa Loorya, and Maura Smale. 2000. Excavating Brooklyn, New York's Rural Past: The Hendrick I. Lott Farmstead Project. Paper presented at the Society for Historical Archaeology meeting, Quebec, Canada.

Roberts, William IV. 1993. Draft: The Archaeological Investigation of the Metro-Tech Project, Brooklyn, New York. CEQR no. 82-248. Submitted to Forest City Ratner Companies by Greenhouse Associates. Report on file with the New York City Landmarks Preservation Commission.

Rockman [Wall], Diana, Wendy Harris, and Jed Levin. 1983. The Archaeological Investigation of the Telco Block, South Street Seaport Historic District, New York, New York. Report on file with the New York City Landmarks Preservation Commission and the National Register of Historic Places.

Rothschild, Nan A., and Susan A. Dublin. 1985. Metropolitan Technology Center, Brooklyn, New York: Phase I: Cultural Resources Summary. Submitted to McKeown and Franz, Inc. Report on file with the New York City Landmarks Preservation Commission.

Salwen, Bert, Sarah Bridges, and Joel Klein. 1974. An Archaeological Reconnaissance at the Pieter Claesen Wyckoff House, Kings County, New York. *Bulletin, New York State Archaeological Association* 61: 26–38.

Santone, Lenore, and Joel D. Irish. 1997. Buried in Haste: Historic Interments from Governors Island, New York. *North American Archaeologist* 18 (1): 19–39.

Skinner, Alanson. 1915. *The Indians of Manhattan Island and Vicinity.* American Museum of Natural History Guide Leaflet 41, New York.

———. 1919. *Explorations of Aboriginal Sites at Throgs Neck and Clasons Point, New York City.* Contribution from the Museum of the American Indian, Heye Foundation, V (4), New York.

———. 1920. *Archaeological Investigations on Manhattan Island, New York City.* Indian Notes and Monographs 2. Museum of the American Indian, Heye Foundation, New York.

Soil Systems. 1982. Proposed Federal Building, Jamaica, New York; Cultural Resource Plan and Scope of Work. For the General Services Administration, Region 2. Report on file with the New York City Landmarks Preservation Commission.

———. 1983. Phase II Archaeological Investigations, Proposed Social Security Administration Building, Jamaica, Queens County, New York. Report on file with the New York City Landmarks Preservation Commission.

Solecki, Ralph. 1986. New York City Archaeology and the Works of Robert Moses. *Professional Archaeologists of New York City Newsletter* 29:15–16.

Staples, Brent. 2001. To Be a Slave in Brooklyn. *New York Times Magazine*, June 24.

Stone, Linda. 1997. Report of Archaeological Testing in Advance of Improvements Associated with the Fence Project at Rufus King Park, Jamaica Ave at 150–153 Streets, Jamaica, Queens, NY. For Gazebo Contracting, Inc. Report on file with the New York City Landmarks Preservation Commission.

———. 1998. Report on Archaeological Testing in Advance of Improvements Associated with the Drainage and Termite Project at Rufus King Park, Jamaica Avenue at 150–153rd Streets, Jamaica, Queens, New York. Prepared for Fredante Construction Company. Report on file with the New York City Landmarks Preservation Commission.

Trelease, Allen W. 1960. *Indian Affairs in Colonial New York: The Seventeenth Century*. Cornell University Press, Ithaca.

Ultan, Lloyd. 1993. *The Bronx in the Frontier Era: From the Beginning to 1696*. Kendall Publishing, Dubuque, Iowa.

Van der Donck, Adriaen. 1968. *A Description of the New Netherlands*, ed. T. F. O'Donnell. Syracuse University Press, Syracuse, N.Y.

Van Wyck, Frederick. 1924. *Keskachauge or The First White Settlement on Long Island*. G. P. Putnam's Sons, New York.

Wall, Diana. 2000. Twenty Years After: Re-Examining Archaeological Collections for Evidence of New York City's Colonial African Past. *African American Archaeology* 28: 1–6.

White, Norval, and Elliot Willensky. 1978. *AIA Guide to New York City*. Collier Books, New York.

White, Shane. 1991. *Somewhat More Independent*. University of Georgia Press, Athens.

Winter, Frederick A. 1981. Excavating New York: Brooklyn. *Archaeology* 34 (1): 56–58.

Illustration Credits

Courtesy African Burial Ground: figs. 2.20, 2.21

Courtesy of the Division of Anthropology, American Museum of Natural History: figs. 4.3, 4.4 (neg. no. 338948, copied by J. Beckett), 5.5

Courtesy American Museum of Natural History Library: figs. 4.11 (neg. no. 24449, photo by W. L. Calver), 4.12

Adapted from Edwards and Emery, 1977, copyright 1977 New York Academy of Sciences, U.S.A.: fig. 1.11

Reprinted by permission of AP/Wide World Photos: fig. 1.7

Adapted from Bolton, 1922, courtesy Bill Nelson: fig. 8.3

From Bolton, 1934: fig. 5.8

From Robert Bolton, Jr., *A History of the County of Westchester from Its First Settlement to the Present Time* (New York: Alexander and Gould, 1848): Fig. 5.11

Courtesy of Brooklyn College Archaeological Research Center (BC-ARC): figs. 8.4, 8.9

Courtesy of The Brooklyn Historical Society: figs. 2.2, 8.6

Courtesy of Anne-Marie Cantwell: fig. 3.3

Courtesy of Columbia University Dept. of Anthropology, William Duncan Strong Museum: fig. 2.6

Adapted from Cornelius Corneliszoon's 1593 patent drawing of a wind-powered sawmill: fig. 1.5

From Fitts and Klein, 2000, reproduced courtesy of John Milner Associates, Inc., and Mattone Group Jamaica Co., L.L.C.: figs. 6.5, 6.6, 6.7, 6.8, 6.9

From Fitts, Klein, and Milne, 2000, reproduced courtesy of John Milner Associates, Inc., and the New York State Dormitory Authority: fig. 6.4

From Fitts and Yamin, 1996, reproduced courtesy of John Milner Associates, Inc., and Atlantic Housing Corporation: figs. 7.4, 7.5

Reprinted courtesy of Joan H. Geismar: fig. 2.13

Courtesy of Joan H. Geismar; photo by Timothy Dalal: fig. 3.2

Courtesy of Joan H. Geismar; photo by Daniel Mayers: fig. 7.6

Courtesy of Edith Gonzalez de Scollard: fig. 8.10

Courtesy of Dr. R. M. Gramly; artist William Parsons: fig. 1.13

Adapted from Haviland and Power, 1994: fig. 5.9

Courtesy of Herbert C. Kraft: fig. 1.12

Reproduced from a lithograph, in the collection of Herbert C. Kraft, from the series by Thomas L. McKenney and James Hall, *The Indian Tribes of North America* (Philadelphia: E. C. Biddle, 1857): fig. 8.8

Museum of the City of New York, Gift of the Department of Parks, 43.165B: fig. 1.2

Courtesy of National Archives and Records Administration: fig. 1.8

Courtesy, National Museum of the American Indian, Smithsonian Institution: figs. 4.2, 4.10, 5.2, 5.3, 5.6, 5.7, 5.10, 8.5

Courtesy Bill Nelson: figs. 1.1, 1.5, 1.9, 2.1, 3.1, 4.1, 5.1, 6.1, 7.1, 8.1

Courtesy of the New York City Landmarks Preservation Commission: fig. 2.18

Courtesy New York City Municipal Archives: figs. 3.12, 7.3, 7.7, 8.2

Collection of The New-York Historical Society: figs. 2.11 (slide no. 1907.32), 2.19 (neg. no. 2731), 3.9 (neg. no. 74146), 4.5 (neg. no. 37775), 4.6 (neg. no. 76108 D), 4.7 (acc. no. 1919.4), 4.8 (neg. no. 76113 D), 4.9 (neg. nos. 76110 D, 76111 D, and 76112 D)

NPS photo by Brett Seymour: fig. 1.10

I. N. Phelps Stokes Collection, Miriam and Ira D. Wallach Division of Art, Prints and Photographs, The New York Public Library, Astor, Lenox, and Tilden Foundations: fig. 6.2

Courtesy of PAL, Pawtucket, Rhode Island: figs. 1.4, 1.6

Courtesy of the Queens Borough Public Library, Long Island Division, Illustrations Collection: fig. 6.3

Reprinted courtesy of Robbins Museum of Archaeology at the Massachusetts Archaeological Society: fig. 5.4

Reprinted by permission of The Society for Historical Archaeology: fig. 2.7

Reprinted by permission of The Society for Historical Archaeology from *Historical Archaeology* 35 (4): 111: fig. 1.3

Courtesy Society for the Preservation of Weeksville and Bedford-Stuyvesant History: fig. 7.2

Courtesy of the South Street Seaport Museum: figs. 2.3, 2.4, 2.5, 2.8, 2.9, 2.10, 2.12, 2.14

Courtesy of the South Street Seaport Museum; photo Diana Wall: figs. 3.6, 3.7, 3.8

The State Museum of Pennsylvania, Pennsylvania Historical and Museum Commission (photo courtesy of New Jersey State Museum): fig. 8.7

Courtesy of Mary Traester: frontispieces for tours 1, 2, 4, 5, 7, and 8

Courtesy U.S. General Services Administration: 2.16, 2.17

Courtesy of Diana Wall: frontispiece for tour 3, 3.4, 3.5, 3.10, 3.11, frontispiece for tour 6, 6.10

Index

Page numbers in italics refer to illustrations.

tableware artifacts: Chinese style, *67*, 67–68; English earthenware, 67, *67*; Gothic style, *62*, 63, 64, 68, 74; Italianate style, 64, *65*, 68; social position and, 156–58, *157–58*

Telco Block site, *42*, 42–43

Teunissen, Tobias, house of, 96, 97, 100

Thompson, Edward, 15

Throckmorton, John, 117

Throgs Neck, 114, 117, 118

Tienhoven, Cornelis van, property of, 29–31, *30*, *31*

Tienhoven, Lucas van, 29

Tijger (ship), 4, *5*

Tompkins, Daniel, 72

Tompkins Square Park, 72

Tredwell family, 68–69, 70

Tweed Courthouse, 47, 48

Uncommon Ground (Ferguson), 38

Underhill, John, 105

Unearthing Gotham (Wall and Cantwell), ix

urbanization, xii, 55, 77, 176, 187

Van Brunt, Jane, 159

Vanderbilt family, 71

Van der Donck, Adriaen, 103, 105

Van Sicklen Cemetery (Brooklyn), 173

Van Voorhis, Daniel, 39

Veindovi, Chief, 165–66

Verrazano Narrows Bridge, 19

Waldron, Rebecca, 100

Wall, Diana: Greenwich Village sites and, 60, 63, 69, 70; lower Manhattan sites and, 31, 34, 36, 38, 42

Wall Street district, xiii

Wampage, 122–23

wampum, 30, *112*, 113, 121, 122

War of *1812*, 4, 7, 163

Warren family, 57, 61

Washington Square, 55, 57, 58, 59, 64–65

Washington Square (James), 64

waterfronts: Brooklyn, 149; Cruger's Wharf, 34–35, *35*; Dutch and English systems compared, 35; Queens, 127

Weeks, James, 150

Weeksville (Brooklyn), 147, 150–52, *151*

Weir Creek, 113, *119*, 119–22, *120*, 181

West Village, 55, 58

whale bones, 116

Whitestone Bridge, 111, 114

Wiechquaskect, x

Wiesniewski, Stanley, 105, 110, 178

Williams, Lt. Col. Jonathan, 3, 4, 5, 7

Williamsburg (Brooklyn), 166–67

Winans, Anthony, 37, 39

windmill, on Governors Island, 7, 8–9, *8–9*

wine bottles, 47, 141, *141*

Winter, Frederick, 171, 173, 176, 177

Woodland peoples, x, 7–8, 114, 115; in Bronx, 103, 105, 110, 114; in Brooklyn, 179; burial sites of, 116; contact with Europeans, 118; Dutch windmill built on land of, 10; on Liberty Island, 10, 12; in northern Manhattan, 79–80, 83; pottery of, *95*, 95–96; in southern Brooklyn, 176; weapons of, 120–21, *121*. See also Native Americans

World Trade Center, 3, 36, 46

World War I, 164

World War II, 17, 164, 174

Wyckoff family, 179

Wyckoff House Museum (Brooklyn), 185–87, *187*

Yamin, Rebecca, 44, 45

yellow fever epidemics, 57